Reputation
MARKETING

Reputation MARKETING

Building and Sustaining Your Organization's Greatest Asset

Joe Marconi

AM AMERICAN MARKETING ASSOCIATION

McGraw-Hill

Chicago   New York   San Francisco   Lisbon   London   Madrid   Mexico City
Milan   New Delhi   San Juan   Seoul   Singapore   Sydney   Toronto

Library of Congress Cataloging-in-Publication Data

Marconi, Joe.
    Reputation marketing : building and sustaining your organization's greatest asset
        p.   cm. (American Marketing Association)
    ISBN 0-658-01429-3
    1. Corporate image.   2. Corporations—Public relations.   3. Brand name
products—Marketing.   I. Title.

HD59.2.M374   2001
659.2'85—dc21   2001040327

McGraw-Hill

A Division of The **McGraw·Hill** *Companies*

1 2 3 4 5 6 7 8 9 0   LBM/LBM   0 9 8 7 6 5 4 3 2 1

ISBN 0-658-01429-3

This book was set in New Caledonia
Printed and bound by Lake Book Manufacturing

Interior design by Jeanette Wojtyla

McGraw-Hill books are available at special quantity discounts to use as premiums and sales promotions, or for use in corporate training programs. For more information, please write to the Director of Special Sales, Professional Publishing, McGraw-Hill, Two Penn Plaza, New York, NY 10121-2298. Or contact your local bookstore.

This book is printed on acid-free paper.

For Todd and Kristin and Emily,
and for Karin

Contents

Acknowledgments

For assistance and support in bringing this book along, thanks to John Nolan, Danielle Egan-Miller, Katherine Hinkebein, and Denise Betts, and at the American Marketing Association, Francesca Van Gorp Cooley. Thanks to Lonny Bernardi, Richard Girod, and Guy Kendler; and with immeasurable appreciation to Karin Gottschalk Marconi for this, our ninth collaboration.

Introduction

Reputation marketing has emerged as an area of specialization among public-relations professionals and marketing consultants. A closer look at the subject reveals marked similarities to the practice of corporate-image management, and in some instances, brand management as well. Are these distinctions important? To some people, perhaps not. But they are distinctions worth knowing and understanding. These are times of unprecedented competition and soaring costs; once an objective is clearly defined and resources are committed to meeting that objective, the strategy and tactics should follow a straight line and remain as focused as possible.

Given that reputation management is a form of public relations, and public relations is part of the field of marketing, how and where does reputation management fit into the marketing plan? Is reputation marketing a viable approach?

This book sets up a number of marketing issues and challenges and examines them from a reputation-specific perspective. How did the marketing work? Sometimes corporate-image marketing techniques benefit a brand or product's reputation, sometimes not. We will note the distinctions and begin to understand that *image*, *brand*, and *reputation* are not the same, and that the terms should not be used interchangeably if a strategy is to achieve its objective.

The public is exposed to a myriad of images and brand-marketing messages every day. This same public forms perceptions of a brand that are based (in part) on the brand's image, and sometimes on its reputation, and makes its decisions accordingly. Marketers need to know what factors are considered in these decisions.

For purposes of this work, let us consider reputation management and reputation marketing as one process. This is not a great leap, since under most circumstances managing and marketing are indeed wholly linked.

A product's image in the marketplace is often enough to determine its success or failure. In today's media-intensive environment, images can be created virtually overnight with an advertising blitz, a highly promoted event, a well-managed cover story, or a prime-time appearance. Building a reputation takes longer, and cannot be bought for the cost of an advertisement. This is a key point that marketers must understand: making an impression and building a reputation are not the same thing.

Many companies and individuals are increasingly using their reputations as marketing tools. Such a strategy is possible in part because technology has evolved; the power of the media can be directed toward creating, changing, shaping, and influencing perceptions in a more narrowly defined context. This means reputations can be created more rapidly, though still not as instantaneously as images or impressions.

The same process, alas, can work in reverse. A reputation that has been carefully nurtured and protected for a century or more can be attacked with enough force to put it into free fall, threatening to undo a long and distinguished history of accomplishment and goodwill.

Reputation Marketing is a guide to creating a focused brand or corporate public-relations philosophy, as well as a plan of action. Each chapter includes specific examples and case references that illustrate the premise of that chapter. This book is intended for marketers, but the information and examples presented here should be equally valuable to service providers, agents, managers, lawyers, and many of the folks in the front office—and the back office as well.

A reputation, good or bad, casts a shadow far and wide that can help or hurt a company or brand. Reputations can affect the bottom line—in every sense of the term. This is about recognizing that fact and making a difference.

Reputation MARKETING

CHAPTER ONE

Who Do You Think You Are?

Understanding Reputation Marketing

The reputation of a man is like his shadow, gigantic when it precedes him, and pygmy in its proportions when it follows.
—Talleyrand

A name, or a single word, can suggest an image. It can speak volumes to us in terms of our beliefs and perceptions. Your target audience may be made up of housewives, students, corporate executives, or securities analysts, but all these groups are "consumers" who act upon what they have seen, heard, and learned. We make our decisions in no small part on impressions—sometimes first impressions, sometimes a series of impressions created over a lifetime, and sometimes impressions that were formed after reading persuasive research. An authoritative research report that begins with a phrase such as, "The company (or product or chief executive) has an excellent reputation," has already colored and shaped all that will follow.

What Is *Reputation Marketing*?

The word *reputation* is not usually misunderstood. *Webster's New World Dictionary* defines *reputation* as (1) the regard, favorable or not, shown for a person or thing by the public, community, and so forth; (2) such regard when favorable (for example, *to lose one's reputation*); or (3) distinction.

Nurturing, protecting, or exploiting a reputation can be a difficult art; the skill with which it is done often determines whether a given company, product, or brand will succeed or fail. Because marketing is, in the broadest sense, about positioning, packaging, pricing, and promotion, managing a reputation is an essential part of the marketing process.

Reputation management is a very focused and specialized practice in and of itself; it goes beyond the routine public-relations and investor-relations functions that have been the standard for decades. A quick Internet search will turn up many public-relations firms that offer *only* reputation-management services.

Additionally, the singular-focus magazine called *Reputation Management* has established itself within the public-relations profession as a highly useful and respected journal with an increasing degree of influence. The magazine's publisher defines reputation management as (1) a counseling discipline that recognizes the importance of reputation as an organizational asset and seeks to ensure that management decisions are taken in an environment in which reputational implications are fully understood, evaluated, and considered so that an organization's behavior earns it a strategically appropriate reputation with important stakeholders; and (2) a results-oriented management function that seeks to leverage reputation as an asset, enlisting important stakeholder groups, including employees, consumers, communities, and investors, to assist the organization in the achievement of its strategic design, and seeking to minimize the resistance of those groups to legitimate management objectives.

Whew!

As definitions go, that one would certainly qualify as being "encompassing"—perhaps too much so. Edelman Public Relations Worldwide, a well-recognized and powerful global PR firm that takes this subject very seriously, has a somewhat more concise overview: "Reputation management is the orchestration of discreet initiatives designed to promote and protect one of the company's most important assets—its corporate reputation—and to help shape an effective corporate image."

The Edelman approach uses a formulation that includes strategic recommendations for crisis management, media relations, philanthropy, influence outreach, corporate advertising, employee relations, sponsorship, and CEO positioning, in an effort to effectively—and strategically—manage a company's corporate image. The Edelman agency's clients are major companies, institutions, and brands, but one can easily make a case for reputation management as a viable approach even when the "product" is intangible: a cause, a public figure, a celebrity, or a politician.

Consider the circumstances under which a reputation can be created, changed, and used to influence consumers, investors, competitors, and the media, used as a consideration in recruiting, or even used to position a company for possible sale or acquisition.

Virtually all marketing revolves around (1) a plan and (2) a USP, or unique selling point. For the purposes of this work, we will focus only on the aspects of the USP that relate to the subject's reputation. In an environment that's crowded with brands, products, companies, and people, what or whom do we admire, like, respect, trust, appreciate, or just *feel good* about? What stands out when the subject is viewed among competitors or others in the same field?

Reputations and Trends

Marketing is routinely credited or blamed for creating trends, but just as often, marketers are required to react, or to *follow* trends created by others. In such instances, reputations can be either enhanced or diminished, sometimes significantly. An old expression in business admonishes, "If you can't be the first, be the best." More than a few late arrivals to the marketplace have had to set that as their goal.

At the very least, it is important to create a *perception* of being the best. If your company isn't the one offering the product that was first in the market, or your company or product was not the first to be successful in a category, the assumption is that you are at a disadvantage. This can be especially humiliating for a market leader, if it is upstaged by a smaller or lesser-known company that brings the product to market first. The market leader has to uphold its reputation and is forced to respond.

Maybe not. The opportunity exists to expand, introduce, or position a product as a significantly better version of the first product. The improved entry may even change the direction of a trend.

Consider how many (or how few) people can tell you who created the first wristwatch, ballpoint pen, pair of eyeglasses, or slip-on shoes. The truth is that it doesn't matter. The people who made these items famous improved on existing products. In the process, they rendered their predecessors less relevant, and altered the course of function and fashion in their respective industries so much that today, any number of creative competitors are regarded as leading brand names. The reputation for quality and style went to the companies that had the best products, not necessarily those that had the first.

Some people dismiss Seattle's Best Coffee as a Starbucks wannabe, which copies the Starbucks marketing and distribution concept—and even the coffee's taste. But by positioning its brand as an acquired taste, "not for everyone," Seattle's Best Coffee offered itself as an *alternative*, setting the bar at a level that does not require it to overtake Starbucks in order to make a respectable showing in terms of market share, pricing, distribution, or advertising.

Perhaps one of the worst accusations against a marketer is that he or she is out of touch with prevailing trends, styles, or fashions. To not understand what is controlling the market at any given point in time calls into question the very need for marketers to exist at all.

The marketer's role is to create distinctions within the competitive environment. This requires an ability to recognize and understand the mood and characteristics of that market. More so now than at any other time, the challenge to "lead, follow, or get out of the way" is a pivotal consideration in the marketplace.

Knowing vs. Thinking

Knowing as much as you can about your market is extremely important, but it is only the first step in becoming market-ready. It is also important to know where you fit in—to *really* know and not simply *think* that you know. Don't fall into the trap of regarding personal opinions or beliefs as knowledge, and intuition as skill. Opinions and intuition can be valuable assets, but do not confuse those qualities with definitive research data.

It took awhile for much of the business community to recognize that research was not a superfluous item on the budget. Companies and professionals are finally beginning to appreciate the importance of separating facts—in the form of timely market research—from the opinions of the CEO's barber, car pool, or mother-in-law. As time goes on, spokespersons in public and corporate life are increasingly announcing that a given thing is what people want, need, or are demanding, only to suffer embarrassment or financial loss for basing such announcements on little more than their personal opinions. And their reputations suffer as well, because they are then described as being out of touch.

The practice of marketing has become more focused, and certain aspects of it can take on greater importance under specific circumstances. For example, a bold use of color in packaging can make a product, company logo, or corporate-identity program appear fresh and more contemporary. But if a more conservative fashion currently dominates the landscape, the very same use of color can appear hopelessly out-of-date. Graphics that suggest a nostalgic, "retro" look might convey a sentimental or emotional appeal—particularly to members of a certain generation—while a design treatment with harder, sharp-edged graphics would appear more futuristic and evoke an entirely different feeling. These cosmetic touches can help define a message that supports a company's desired reputation.

Public figures are increasingly marketed through ghostwritten books or autobiographies, videos, films, CDs, posters, newsletters, websites, lines of clothing, even foods and fragrances. These are products, but they are also intended as "reputation builders."

Merchandising a Reputation

Consider the film star Paul Newman's line of branded food products, Newman's Own, which markets popcorn, lemonade, pasta sauce, and ice cream, among other items. Mr. Newman is widely known for donating the profits from the company bearing his name to various charities. But such a strategy might not be commercially viable if Mr. Newman did not already have a reputation as a social and political activist *before* undertaking this venture.

Another example that stands apart from the more common type of celebrity endorsement is that of the Kennedy family. The late president and Mrs. Kennedy, over the space of four decades, were merchandised on virtually everything from pens, coffee mugs, and money clips to books, films, videos, action figures, fashion dolls, and calendars. These merchandising possibilities were extended to virtually any member of the family and every generation, where reputations may seem fixed or enigmatic. A bust or souvenir plate of President Kennedy may not seem unusual. But replicas of Mrs. Kennedy's bridal gown, or the use of her image as the model for a line of collectible dolls, illustrated a unique merchandising campaign. Books of paper dolls with several changes of clothes were created around the Kennedy children. The Kennedys' glamourous image and reputation were the basis for all their merchandising.

A review by Professor Todd Gitlan of a book about the late Senator Robert F. Kennedy, the president's brother, focuses on the way that a reputation can define a subject. He notes, "The cliches start with the romantic, schemer and fixer. We know RFK for McCarthyism, ruthlessness, family devotion and doom, hubris, loyalty, passion, calculations, recklessness, moral advance through seasoning, grief, hesitation, missed opportunities, malevolent destiny, martyrdom. Notice how many of these features seem to cancel each other out."

Indeed.

The book described in the review reached the *New York Times* bestseller list shortly after its publication. Such is the marketing value of an image and reputation—even one that seems so contradictory.

Certain musical performers draw crowds to their concerts as much for their identification with particular social, political, or environmental causes as for their musical talent. People support performers who have a reputation for supporting issues the people themselves care about. And more cynically, companies that sponsor charity drives or cause-related events frequently do so for the sole purpose of generating goodwill and a positive corporate image.

Treating a Reputation as an Asset

Reputation marketing can be found in most successful marketing efforts, even if the process is not described as such. Look again at the lengthy definition of reputation management offered by *Reputation Management* magazine. The word *asset* appears twice. In business, across the full spectrum of products, services, and intellectual property, a company's management and marketing go hand in hand. How people regard it is its asset.

An "asset" cannot be managed to its fullest potential without consideration for marketing at all levels (labor and management) and in all its characteristics (pricing, promotion, positioning, and distribution). Marketing is so critical a part of the production process that it cannot be separated from the asset at any stage.

Knowledge is power, but knowledge is never the result of guessing or following your gut. How much does the public (or target audience) know about the asset? How much does the marketer know? How much does the marketer *think* the target audience knows, and how much do they know for sure?

This goes directly to the central question of this chapter, "Who do you think you are?" It's a question that must be taken seriously. Companies all too often become so internally focused that their perceptions of their place and importance to the market are out of sync with reality.

After many years of hesitation, research tools like opinion polls, surveys, and focus groups are finally gaining influence with many of the top companies of the world. Very often, however, marketers (as with CEOs) are accused of disregarding or dismissing the results of such efforts when the conclusions don't say what management wants them to say.

The likely reason for this is not just a matter of wanting one's own way (although that can certainly be a factor), but because a marketing plan exists and has existed for so long that it's considered "the way the company operates." Some might even say it defines the company's reputation. Making changes in such a plan in order to follow the conclusions of market research may not only be costly, but can represent a significant departure from established practices. It is sometimes viewed as more prudent and less costly—and less threatening—to simply set aside such conclusions and recommendations with dismissive comments like "I don't believe the survey results" or "I know my market better than some focus group." Such a position, even when advanced by an experienced and seasoned member of an organization, can be dangerous as well as expensive.

Listen to Your Heart . . . but Rely on the Research

It is important to consider all sides of the issue. Certainly, despite its increasingly scientific methods, research can indeed be imperfect. A marketer might wisely attempt to validate research with additional analysis or comparisons with trade-group data. As successful as their "gut feelings" may have been over the years, even casino dealers in Las Vegas understand that there is more to the science of winning than instinct.

Tastes change, often very rapidly. Sometimes promoting a trend or product, particularly in a high-tech environment where anything might be designated as "the next big thing," requires flexibility and rapid changes of direction on the part of marketers. This flexibility is at odds with the long-held marketing principle of having a solid plan and sticking to it. That principle makes good sense theoretically, but inflexibility is a reflection of poor planning and an unwillingness to remain competitive in a changing marketplace.

A rumor circulated on the Internet can be picked up by the media anywhere in the world, causing opinions to change instantly and dramatically. A marketing plan must be timely and have the flexibility to anticipate "worst-case scenarios," and then be able to moderate or change in order to protect the reputations involved.

Heightened concern for conservation and pressures from special-interest environmental groups can require marketers to be more or less aggressive in their efforts at a given point in time. Again, it is a matter of checking the pulse of the market and being responsive to it.

It is generally conceded that in the United States, people are more litigious than in other markets of the world. A CEO or board of directors must have a well-defined crisis management plan ready, should circumstances require its being put into effect. Quite often in matters of litigation, a company's reputation becomes the main focus (offensively or defensively) of its case. In this regard, reputation management has emerged as an important factor in positioning a company or product at every stage of its development, evolution, and maintenance—and validating the strength of its position with research.

The public is accustomed to hearing advertisers stake their reputation on claims of quality or value. Implied in such statements is the recognition that one's reputation is an asset important enough to have real value as a "stake." In reality, one's reputation is *always* tied to such claims as a matter of course, but the very act of verbalizing the promise and advertising it in this way is intended to give added weight to the reputation, defining it as if it were a negotiable commodity. Managers routinely justify decisions by noting that they "have a reputation to protect."

But do they? Sometimes there are exceptions to a rule.

Businesses of all sizes, from a professional-services firm run by a single person to a large, publicly traded company, can become so caught up in their own affairs that they fail to see (or accept) how they are perceived by the outside world. If that outside world should happen to include customers, prospective customers, investors, and regulators, such failures of perception could affect critical decisions and alter the company's future.

A consultant was overheard telling a friend that his young company was "getting a reputation for being expensive, but good."

After a pause, the friend replied, "Well, I've heard about half of your reputation."

The consultant was, of course, describing the reputation he *wanted* to have and what he was hoping people were thinking about his company—that he was the Rolls-Royce of new consulting firms—though in fact he didn't have the slightest idea of what people were *really* saying about his company.

Does it always matter?

Some executives say they've got more business than they can handle. There are certainly some commodities that are so in demand that businesses who traffic in them thrive, despite the arrogant or bumbling actions of their representatives. A toy merchant had a product that was so popular for several seasons that he would repeatedly, blatantly push to see how far he could go before customers revolted. This toy marketer manipulated his most loyal customers, charging "collector's prices" for the latest edition of his toy and promising to "retire" each new product shortly after its introduction. His tactics and his seeming indifference to the concerns of his customers and vendors, while criticized openly by some members of the media, were tolerated by a constituency that just wanted the toy, no matter what. The product's popularity ran its course and today some would say it's not worth beans, though the toymaker's name remains on *Forbes* magazine's list of the richest people in America.

There is also the now-classic example of the oil company we will simply call Company "XX." On a particular occasion, one of its tankers despoiled a national coastline with a spill that poured thousands of gallons of oil over a large, biodiverse area. The company sought to shrug off the incident and avoided taking any responsibility in the matter. Although people around the world expressed their outrage at such an offensive response to an environmental disaster, the company's position in the marketplace remained strong and its market share stood relatively undiminished. People needed the oil.

On a much lighter note, a classic episode of the hit TV series *Seinfeld* featured a character dubbed "The Soup Nazi." This eccentric genius of a chef was known for being rude, insulting, and intimidating to customers, yet his soups were so good that people stood in lines and tolerated the abuse he heaped on them. Just TV fiction? Not at all. The character is based on an actual soup chef, well known for his rudeness and eccentricity—and his extremely successful business.

So it would seem that it is indeed possible to have a terrible reputation and a good business at the same time.

Did the people who ran the businesses in these three examples care if they had bad reputations? It would seem not. It could be said, however, that they're among the very limited number of exceptions to the following generally accepted belief: a company cannot show prolonged indifference to its customers, or engage in ritual bad behavior, without eventually seeing its business suffer. The public waits and watches for these "bad apples" to fall so they can hear about someone who got what he or she deserved.

A company with a good reputation (and a management team of at least average intelligence) wants to preserve that reputation, recognizing its value with customers, investors, employees, and even with competitors. Recruiting efforts, mergers and acquisitions, trade-association activities, and a regulatory environment are all heavily influenced by reputation.

Reputations in Good Times and Bad

In an earlier book, *Crisis Marketing*, I dealt with the issue of "when bad things happen to good companies." The subject is always timely, as businesses continue to recognize their areas of vulnerability and develop plans to deal with them. Any business, regardless of size or industry, must accept that sometimes things may very well go wrong.

Stories abound of companies that "took the hit" or "dodged the bullet"—meaning that they survived an unwelcome situation that could have crippled or destroyed their business. Some companies actually come out of such situations stronger than before, using the crisis situation to demonstrate their ability to cope well with adversity, and enhancing their reputations in the process. Others are not so fortunate:

- An airline was forced to discontinue its operations following the crash of one of its planes. Its reputation was devastated because of the way it handled the media and the victims' families. The rest of its business collapsed a short time later.

   Clearly, a crash, with its ensuing loss of many lives, is about the worst type of problem an airline can have. Yet other airlines had experienced such disasters—some of them several times—and not only remained operational, but retained the goodwill of air travelers and the general public, who seemed willing to accept that such tragedies do indeed happen and that business must go on.

■ A fast-food restaurant was sent reeling out of control (and out of most U.S. markets) when several of its customers reportedly became ill as a result of eating contaminated meat the restaurant had served.

Another fast-food chain was charged with being a supporter of the Church of Satan. But the latter company's customers just sighed and ordered extra cheese on their quarter-pounders.

Why such loyalty to one burger chain, but not the other? Or to one airline and not another?

Some people might conclude that it is simply a case of ValuJet not being American Airlines or TWA, and of Jack in the Box not being McDonald's. While that could be true, behind such loyal sentiments also lie a recognition and an appreciation of the overall reputation for integrity of one company over another, a reputation that promises a commitment to quality and customer service. The favored companies can also take credit for having effectively communicated their stories to the public.

In his book *Value-Added Public Relations*, the highly respected public-relations expert Thomas L. Harris writes, "McDonald's is dedicated to earning its customers' trust. . . . [The company's] community involvement programs span the country and the globe." He cites the philosophy of McDonald's founder Ray Kroc, which holds that those who take money out of the community have a responsibility to give something back. Mr. Harris points out that McDonald's "long had been a committed, involved, and visible community citizen," *before* trouble broke out in a particular community. Other businesses were trashed, yet McDonald's was left alone. The reason was credited to the McDonald's policy that required the corporation as a whole, *and* each of its individual locations, to be "committed, involved, and visible community citizens," and the fact that this policy was known to the restaurant's customers and other members of the community.

With all due respect to companies and individuals who choose to make anonymous contributions to worthy causes, and to do good works and deeds without asking for attention, *snap out of it!*

McDonald's and thousands of other businesses have learned that a good reputation in a community doesn't come from keeping good works a secret. And in a crisis situation, whether it is a slightly publicized nuisance lawsuit brought by a disgruntled employee or a well-publicized charge of discrimination, the company that is known for being a good corporate citizen—that is, known for believing it has an obligation to "give something back" to the community—is far better positioned to receive a favorable outcome than the company that didn't seem to care much about the community or (worse yet) cared but didn't want anyone to know about it.

Still worse is not even knowing whether the people of the community *think* you care. Knowing how your company and its people are perceived is directly related to the basic question of whether people will want to do business with you.

A business that maintains it does not need to conduct even basic attitude and awareness research is operating on assumptions that may not be correct. The potential mistaken assumptions could result in costs far greater than that of any poll or survey.

An important distinction exists, however, between acknowledging good deeds and grandstanding. A public-relations professional understands this distinction and craft the story with sufficient humility and subtlety as to *enhance* the quality of the deed.

It is just good business to take credit for benevolent deeds done in the name of the business, its employees, and its investors. It is also good business to let the news get around sooner rather than later.

It is *not* good for business if the first time a community (or the public at large) becomes aware of a company is when that company is at the center of a controversy or a negative news story.

First impressions still count for a lot. It is far more difficult to *change* someone's perception—particularly a negative perception—than it is to create an impression in the first place. Bad news stays in people's minds longer than good news, and most folks don't want to admit that they misjudged; they prefer not to reconsider opinions that have already been formed.

Consider the family-restaurant chain that, if it was known for anything at all from its advertising and marketing, was known as an inexpensive place to eat. Its first real taste of national news came when the restaurant was accused of having a policy of racial discrimination against its customers. The company's lawyers, who seemed to be totally unskilled in public relations, issued a series of denials that managed to keep the stories on the nightly newscasts far longer than was necessary. People who had never patronized the restaurant chain now told reporters that they never would, since even a suspicion that the company or its managers had a racial bias was enough to justify passing it by. Even worse, this seemed to be the only time most people could remember hearing the company's name mentioned on the news.

And what about the restaurant chain's employees at all of the chain's locations across the country? They were all—regardless of their individual beliefs, associations, and personal histories—affected by the accusations. To have to deny a charge of racism puts an employee (and the company itself) in an unmanageable position. It's like the old question, Are you still beating your wife? There is no answer that erases the doubt. Good employees deserve better than to be put in such a position.

After the fact, a public apology from a corporate spokesperson (which by its nature acknowledges, *at the very least*, the *appearance* of inappropriate business conduct) can be too little, too late in terms of the company's public image and reputation. A charge had been made and denied, yet the continuing coverage given to the situation impugned the reputation of restaurants in the chain that were many cities removed from the locations where the incidents were said to have taken place. And every time the company spokesperson made an appearance to refute the charges, he would have to restate them, thereby bringing the story to the attention of all the people who might have missed the charges and denials in previous rounds.

Is this a fair criticism of the restaurant's response? Is it possible to respond to an attack without drawing attention to it?

Certainly, it is a challenge—in this case, one that was not helped by the fact that for years, the company had paid little attention to cultivating a reputation for anything other than offering cheap meals. Many people, including those who ran the company, probably thought that was enough.

They were wrong.

This company, and others who want to avoid situations like this, should have asked themselves the following questions *before* the troubles began. Being able to answer yes to even a few of them could have averted such a meltdown.

- Have we made an effort to determine how we are regarded by our customers and community, if indeed the community thinks about us at all?
- Do we ever try to associate ourselves with our own or another charity?

- Do we have a well-known policy regarding environmental concerns?
- Do we recycle?
- Do we offer discounts to senior citizens and students?
- Do we have a children's menu and give away coloring books or comics that have a safety message?
- Do we pay our employees more than the minimum wage and offer benefits of any kind?
- Do we have "heart-healthy" choices on the menu?
- Is our property a smoke-free environment?
- Do we serve liquor?
- Do we provide for secure or free parking?
- Are our carryout containers recyclable?
- Do we accept major credit cards or bank cards?
- Do our employees wear uniforms?
- Is the company the proud sponsor of, for example, the U.S. Olympic Team? The Special Olympics? United Way? Public television? A local school PTA, learning fair, or Little League program?

Political correctness notwithstanding, these are some of the questions that, when answered, help define whether a business will be considered a "committed, involved, and visible community citizen." And that is what the public should already believe, *before* any bad news becomes a matter of public record.

In the case of our rumor-plagued restaurant chain: did the company's management believe that their restaurants had a reputation of being "cheap, but good"? Or did the company's management never bother to try to find out what the public thought about it, perhaps believing that sales revenue said it all? An effort to find out what people thought could have turned up information that people perceived the restaurant as unfriendly, unwelcoming—perhaps more unwelcoming to some people than others.

It is important to a business's success that it have a good reputation. It is important to know, at the onset, if a company has any reputation at all, and if so, what that reputation is. In the case of the restaurant chain in this example, the fact that it offered cheap meals might have been the last thing it needed to promote.

Who did the company think it was? Did it bother to find out? Does it make a difference? The company will have to answer the first two questions itself. To the third question, the answer is a gigantic *yes*.

SUMMARY OF CHAPTER ONE

- Marketing can move in many directions at many different times, either creating or following trends. Even followers of trends can find opportunities to be competitive, adhering to principles like "If you can't be the first, be the best."
- Reputation management treats a corporate image as an asset—to be shaped, nurtured, protected, and used.
- A common reason for companies to sponsor events is to generate goodwill and a charitable reputation in a community or around the world.
- A company can often become internally focused to such a degree that its own perception of its reputation may not agree with that of the public, or its important market segments.
- It is a sound reputation-management strategy to give something back to the community in which you do business.
- Don't let your benevolent deeds go unnoticed. Anonymous contributions and worthy acts of kindness are not good for business. Modestly take credit for what you do.
- A good reputation is the cornerstone of a successful business.

CHAPTER TWO

Attitudes and Awareness

The Role of Research in Building Your Reputation

A fair reputation is a plant delicate in its nature, and by no means rapid in its growth.
—Jeremy Taylor

Coming into the marketplace with a good reputation is an advantage. People are more inclined to do business with and pledge support to companies they hold in high regard. But in order to achieve this high regard by giving the public what it wants, it is first necessary to know what it wants and target your message accordingly. A part of that message should reflect your ongoing concern for knowing what your target audience wants.

For decades, researchers were regarded as part of that odd group of number crunchers and fact checkers in the basement. They labored over endless questionnaires and compiled lists of boring statistics that were rarely more than footnotes to the annual budget report.

In recent years, however, researchers have emerged as master strategists, with the status and prestige normally accorded to wizards. The boring printouts of numbers are excitedly described as "the pulse of the market."

Research data is often used as a device to influence target audiences. Describing a product as the "fastest-selling" or the "most popular in its category" sends an implied message that anyone who is not a regular user of (or has not at least *tried*) the product is outside of the mainstream—in a culture where acceptance is coveted. If someone has not seen "this summer's hottest film" or has not read "the biggest book of the year," that person has missed something big enough to measure.

Research Can Create Momentum

When you create what used to be called a "bandwagon effect," an expression that described a band on a wagon or truck driving through town to create attention for an event that was following close behind (such as a circus or a rodeo), you generate a momentum and high level of enthusiasm for a subject. It's human nature to want to be accepted, to be "inside the circle." One way to demonstrate insider status is to be aware of what is currently fashionable and establish a relationship with it.

People stand in line to buy whatever toy the media has pronounced the biggest-selling, hottest toy of the season. How do we know that it's been such a high seller? Researchers have polled stores, customers, potential customers, and (often significantly) other researchers, about what they have seen, heard, or believe.

Since the 1990s, tracking polls—snapshots of people's opinions in numerical form—have become increasingly popular, influential, and controversial devices in the political realm for gauging levels of interest and support. A high score in a tracking poll indicates a high level of interest, which is justification for greater media attention.

Star Power Helps Build Reputations

Although tracking polls are perhaps most strongly identified with political matters, consider the news item that tells you a particular television program is expected to be "the sensation of the fall season." How did it achieve that status before its first viewing? Its director or star has a reputation for producing hits.

A new Muppet toy, Star Wars CD-ROM, or Razor scooter is projected to be the bestselling toy this Christmas. Why? Because the creators of these products have a good track record and a reputation for knowing what the public wants. A new movie starring Julia Roberts or Jim Carrey will probably be the summer's blockbuster. Investors, exhibitors, and marketers care less about the film's quality than the reputation of these performers for being able to pull people into theaters—even for less-than-terrific movies.

The initial reports are usually the result of intensive hype and promotional activity, which may or may not reflect actual research. But when the TV show, product, movie, or whatever finally comes to market, the next set of tracking polls will show how successful the product *actually* was. That information, once a mere report to the sales department or CEO, will be interpreted for presentation to the media and reflected in ads. The message will be not so much that the public should try, buy, or see something because it's *good* but because *everybody's talking about it.*

Listening to the Market

Research experts Vincent P. Barabba and Professor Gerald Zaltman, in *Hearing the Voice of the Market*, note that "Data may take many forms: rumors, forecasts, . . . intuitive feelings, personal observations, recommendations, opinions, and almost anything else that purports to describe or relate to a past, current, or future situation. Data are representations of reality that may or may not have meaning, accuracy, or believability."

Researchers make various distinctions, defining data that are clearly understood as *information*, what is not clearly understood as *uninformative*, and a message that is believed and accepted as *intelligence*. The designation received by the data, however, will not necessarily affect its application to the marketing process.

When the narrator of a TV commercial uses a phrase like "Most people know that aspirin can save your life," the advertiser is (1) flattering the audience member for knowing something that, in fact, he or she may not know; (2) providing worthwhile information; and (3) asking the audience to accept two facts: that aspirin can save your life and that most people know this.

Has the advertiser polled "most people"? No. It may be that no evidence exists for the claim. If there is evidence, it will be based on a representative sampling of average people who, when asked if they knew this, answered affirmatively; their answers were generalized to the large mass of society they were asked to represent.

The lack of specifics—not claiming that most nineteen-year-old, Spanish-speaking residents of Texas, for example, knew these facts—is what keeps the advertiser out of trouble. A vagueness and generality, implying widespread support for the claim, has become commonplace.

Hype Statements Aren't Research

When was the last time anyone challenged a politician who used a phrase like "People are sick and tired of . . . (whatever the politician wants to position him- or herself against)"? Such phrases are routinely accepted without challenge; the public assumes that speakers will engage in some degree of hyperbole to make their point.

While obviously such hyperbole is not research, or even taken seriously for the most part, claims of being "the most trusted source for news" or "the choice of a new generation," or references to the mood or the will of "most honest people" do diminish people's respect for much of what *is* offered as research.

Businesses can only afford to take so many chances. Replacing research with hype statements, and then going into a market without basic information about what people think of you or your product, is one chance you cannot afford.

Research must be used. A company that hopes to exploit its record of past successes—its reputation—and learns from attitude and awareness research that few people know or credit the company with those successes, has overestimated its reputation and is setting itself up for a fall if nothing is done about the research results.

Attitudes and Awareness Tell a Story

Attitude and awareness research has long been regarded as pretty basic stuff, by market-research standards. It is often thought of as the "bare minimum" commitment to research that a business should make.

Do people know your company? If so, what do they think of it—both on its own and relative to the competition? What is your

market share? What do people *think* your market share is? How
does this compare with information from another time or a different market cycle?

The answers to these very basic questions can be critical to the
positioning of your product, service, or brand, and most certainly
are important in determining a marketing budget.

To many people, a *better-known* brand is regarded as a
better brand. Awareness brings familiarity, and familiarity brings
acceptance. So a higher level of awareness of a subject translates
to a generally more favorable attitude. And a favorable attitude
over a prolonged period of time is the definition of a good
reputation.

What to Do if What the Public Knows Is Bad

Marketers know, however, that all news is not good news. Consider
the instances where awareness evolves from controversy—such as
a highly publicized crisis—or other negative news. In such cases,
research to determine the attitudes of the public or industry
becomes even more important.

What would an appropriate strategy be if both the good news
and the bad news surrounded a company within the same given
period of time? It could certainly happen.

Consider the case of the multilevel marketer of a popular line
of "nutritional" products. The company enjoyed a highly successful
launch and soaring sales. The products generated great awareness
in media circles, and thus to the general public. The company's
youthful CEO quickly established a reputation for being a charis-
matic speaker who could stir up enthusiasm for the new product
lines.

But not long after the company's successful launch, two national newsweekly magazines ran stories suggesting that an ingredient in the company's bestselling product might be dangerous. Quickly, the high level of awareness turned negative. Despite the company's denials, the public was uncertain about not only that particular product, but other products marketed by the company. The brand took a huge hit because it was still basking in its initial success; the company had greatly overestimated the loyalty of its customer base. Even though it had only been in existence for a relatively short period of time, the company assumed that customers would dismiss the allegations of the media as jealous remarks by competitors and critics. Quite simply, because of its virtually instant success, it had nowhere to go but down.

Attitude and awareness research would have alerted the company's management to the serious damage the bad publicity had done, and to the rather tentative appreciation the public actually had toward the brand. A plan could have been developed, either to correct the problem by removing the ingredient in question or to reassure the marketplace. Perhaps a more long-term plan would have been to shift the marketing emphasis toward some of the company's other—less controversial—products. But by assuming public sentiment was on its side, managers showed an arrogance that proved costly. Instead of being able to exploit the business's former reputation as a hot young company, the managers had to devote their energies for several years to a grudging campaign of damage control and a struggle to hold on to what business remained.

In a situation such as this, two choices exist. Doing nothing and waiting for the problem to simply fade from the public's view (usually the first choice of the folks in the legal department) is not one of them. The first choice—if there actually is a problem with the product's formulation—is to immediately remove that product from the market and heavily publicize the fact that you are doing so in the public interest. Offer a full refund for the return of the unused product and stress in your public statements the number of other products you have, the length of time those products have been around, and the total amount of product sales the company has recorded since its launch. This will put the questionable product in a wider context, which should position the brand overall in a somewhat more positive, safer light.

Please note: If your product is indeed determined to have caused harm, your problem is not a marketing problem and is outside the scope of this material. Lawyers will have to advise you as to the degree of exposure you face.

Your second choice—if the product is *not* dangerous—is to say so, but offer to replace it anyway and suspend sales in the short term, while an independent testing organization evaluates the product and issues a report that will state conclusively that the product is safe. Such actions will (1) benefit your reputation for marketing a safe product, (2) position you as the target or victim of untrue, unfair, and potentially damaging charges, and (3) put you on the record as willing to sustain financial loss in the interests of your customers' health and safety. The product's reintroduction can be publicized as "back by popular demand—proven safe." During the entire period that the charges, evaluation, and reintroduction are going on, stuff your marketing materials with as many testimonials and endorsements as you can from satisfied customers and health-industry professionals. Mention them by name.

In this example, research into the product will determine safety, and *market research* will provide you with the statistical basis for your claims of public acceptance and overall problem-free usage of the product.

Coming Back from a Crisis

Recognize that restoring luster to a tarnished reputation is difficult but not impossible. Once a brand is the subject of controversy, some members of the public (and people within its own industry) will always view it with a degree of suspicion. A good two-prong strategy for dealing with this is (1) to issue research reports that cite surveys of satisfied customers (identified by name); and (2) to designate a spokesperson who will confront the controversy, and in so doing, keep it in context by directly acknowledging either that a problem existed *but it has been corrected* or that a charge was made which was proved conclusively to be false. Invite any lingering questions anyone may have. Emphasize claims of safety and effectiveness on the product packaging and in the marketing materials and advertising.

One important reason why so many products—from aspirin to cold remedies to diet plans—become known as "safe and effective" is that the words "safe and effective" are printed right on the package. The effectiveness of such an approach should not be denied because of its simplicity—indeed, it should be a reminder that creating new, flashy, and futuristic terms is not always the best approach, since often a few simple, understandable words will get the job done.

A strategy such as the one the subject company chose, which ignores or dismisses potentially damaging criticism regardless of its source, based on a belief that no one will likely pay much attention or take the comments seriously, is no strategy at all. It can also be called an act of supreme arrogance; and in this case, it left a very successful company highly damaged and vulnerable.

Marketers who don't maintain an ongoing program of attitude and awareness research to confirm or reveal what particular target audiences think about them are like the traveler who leaves home without bothering to lock the door. It is a very risky position to be in.

Why Research Must Precede the Sales Call

Perhaps one of the most simple, powerful, and direct examples of the importance of reputation marketing is the classic, decades-old magazine ad for (appropriately) McGraw-Hill Magazines. In that ad, a colorless, expressionless, bald, bespectacled, bow tie–wearing sales prospect sits snugly in an old-fashioned office chair as the copy explains:

> "I don't know who you are.
> I don't know your company.
> I don't know your company's product.
> I don't know what your company stands for.
> I don't know your company's customers.
> I don't know your company's record.
> I don't know your company's reputation.
> Now—what is it you wanted to sell me?"

It is fascinating to consider that the ad could be run today without a word of its copy being changed and still make its point just as effectively. Making the sale is an uphill proposition much of the time, even under the best of circumstances. Using valuable sales time to have to first explain who you are, what you do, and why your prospect should care cuts into that time and makes the sale even tougher.

But even worse than having to make explanations is going into the sales meeting without even knowing what—if anything—your prospect thinks of you, your product, company, or industry. This is the equivalent of coming to bat with two strikes against you in the final inning of play. In an era of cost-effective instant communication, this situation does not need to exist.

A company with a good reputation has an edge, but how much of an advantage this affords should never be left to guesswork. Studies of the market, surveys, polls, and focus groups are useful. Additionally, there are a number of frequently overlooked synergistic marketing vehicles that yield important data, such as:

- Guarantees
- Warranties
- Contests
- Sweepstakes
- Discount coupons
- Membership cards
- Credit cards
- Gift certificates
- Service hotlines
- Rebate redemptions

Marketers should know that these ten items were devised as much (or more) to gather information for a database as to actually deliver the identified item, process, or service. These devices provide opportunities to collect information on attitudes and awareness, as well as valuable data such as a customer's age, sex, zip code, interests, and media and shopping preferences. For example, a warranty or guarantee card included with the purchased product is either filled out and returned or it is not. If it is *not*, and the number of cards received is only a minuscule percentage of the total products sold, it is reasonable to conclude that your guarantee or warranty is not a major issue, concern, or commodity of value to the customer. Therefore, discontinuing guarantees on future versions of the product could translate to cost savings (in potential replacement products and repairs) that could be reallocated into something the customer perceives to be of greater importance or value.

If, on the other hand, the document is filled in and returned, it provides not only the information requested, but opportunities for further communication. For example, a letter thanking the customer for purchasing the product could be accompanied by a special limited-edition/limited-time-only sale flyer, offering both heavily discounted and premium-priced items.

A response to this sale flyer not only qualifies the customer as a viable and active purchaser, but also provides insight into the customer's willingness to spend more money on additional purchases and/or premium items. Large orders and/or frequent purchases can be reasonably interpreted as reflective of a favorable attitude toward the company, product, or service. The purchase of gift certificates, whether at full or discounted prices, again suggests a favorable opinion. Lack of response after the purchase can be an indication of either an unfavorable opinion or the need for the company to secure more information. Customers who respond to invitations to sign up for catalogs that offer "special unadvertised sales" or "memberships" that carry discounts and special offers probably have a favorable opinion toward the offering company.

Hyping the Responses

As direct-marketing specialists know, a response rate is appreciably higher when it is tied to an incentive offer (such as a free book or video), a rebate, or a chance to win. Given the countless "free giveaways" that exist, it cannot be assumed that people will respond, or provide you with data, if they don't believe it will somehow accrue to their benefit.

It is truly important to track what is *not* done. Discount coupons never redeemed, gift certificates never cashed, rebate offers that draw little or no response, and contests that draw a very low number of entries may all be due to a combination of factors. But a reasonable person could conclude that, in terms of attitude and awareness research, definitive information is needed on the probable causes of the poor response.

Does a low response indicate a general lack of interest, lack of awareness, or a poorly conceived and badly executed proposition? Does it reflect an unfavorable attitude toward the company—either on its own or relative to competitors? Whether the reason is all of these or none of them, you need to know the answer.

Companies of all sizes manage to come up with creative reasons why they choose not to spend money on attitude and awareness research (and many other types of research as well). Knowing what and if your public thinks of you is one of the most basic steps in running a marketing program.

No company needs a reputation for sidestepping the process that gathers information to keep your company, business, or brand alive.

SUMMARY OF CHAPTER TWO

- Research is more than just the process of gathering and reviewing information; it is a commodity in its own right that can be used to influence target groups.
- A high score in a survey or poll provides marketing information to be released and exploited.

- Attitude and awareness research gives the pulse of the market, revealing what people know and how they feel about a specific subject.
- A better-known brand is regarded as a better brand—*unless* the notoriety derives from negative news stories and perceptions.
- Guarantees, warranties, contests, and credit cards are premiums, promotions, and benefits, but they are also instruments that help marketers keep track of the pulse of the market.
- In order to gauge attitudes and awareness, it is important to track both what is done and what is *not* done by members of a target audience.

CHAPTER THREE

A Long and Distinguished History . . . or Not

Using What You Have (or What You Don't Have) to Manage Your Reputation

Virtue has its own rewards, but has no sale at the box office.

—Mae West

A company's longevity, when considered in terms of its reputation, sometimes presents the proverbial two-sided coin. On the one side, a company that has been around awhile—surviving competitive battles, economic swings, and numerous trend cycles—sends the marketplace a message that its longevity is well earned, that there is a good reason why it is still around. Perhaps it offers higher quality or better distribution or superior service or more value for price.

These factors all benefit the user or consumer, and provide a strong message under any circumstances. Certainly in a business-to-business context, an old, established company conveys through its very existence a sense of stability and the implication that it understands how to do things right. This is important in today's environment, where both businesses and consumers worry that the companies they are dealing with will close their doors or otherwise be unable to fulfill promises. So a reputation for being an old, solid, established company is a good thing, right?

Sometimes.

The other side of the coin is the natural inclination of both consumers and companies to try the newest, freshest version of almost anything. Marketers have effectively conditioned consumers to believe—and in this case, even corporate CEOs and other business decision makers are consumers—that new is good, older is bad. There is often a certain quaint—and dismissive—regard for the dusty antiques that hang in there year after year, who still insist that "the old ones are the best." Whether these beliefs are attributed to the youth culture, the Information Age, or simply the established business practice of always keeping the pipeline filled with "new and improved" versions of whatever is current, they work in the favor of new entrants to the market and force established companies and products to defend themselves.

A successful defense adds to the established company's reputation as a winner. A loss of market share, even a slight one, invites competitors and critics to characterize the established name as being "on the decline," or worse, "the choice of yesterday."

Therefore, companies, businesses, and brands must not only do all they can to create a good reputation for themselves in the marketplace, but should they be fortunate enough to succeed, they must aggressively defend that reputation and justify their leadership position over and over again.

Some of the biggest, most powerful names in business have fallen victim to this quest for "the new thing"—Xerox, General Motors, and Sears are only a few of them. The market asks every day: who will be the next IBM or Apple or Microsoft? Who has built a reputation for being aggressive, innovative, and enormously successful? And who has become the one to beat?

Many people believe that the wisdom of one's "elders," historically regarded as priceless, has been relegated to a place so far back on the sale table that it would have a hard time finding a buyer at any price. In the Internet Age, the focus is less on wisdom than on whatever is newest and flashiest. The "wisdom of the ages" is pretty much what it sounds like: a thing of the past. Even the Internet Age has seen its light begin to dim after only a couple of years.

A company's reputation has always gone hand in hand with its history. But this may no longer be the case. A company that tries to build its advertising campaign, much less its reputation, on the fact that it has been around since 1899 will find that longevity itself is no longer the big selling point it might have been a couple of decades earlier, since few of its original customers are still around and reverence for age is no longer fashionable.

Who cares how long a company has been in business? More specifically, why *should* anyone care?

The answer is that customers, one's industry, regulators, and especially investors should care because when a company has been in business for more than a hundred years, that is an indication that it knows how to be responsive to the needs of its market. In the parlance of an era when people regularly consider each act and reaction and ask, "Is that a good thing or a bad thing?"—*that's a good thing*. This company has survived while others have not. That seems simple enough.

In marketing efforts to build and exploit a company's reputation, the phrase "experience counts" still gets a good workout, as it does in most areas of business and public service. But a distinction must be clearly drawn between the age and experience of a business or corporation and the age and experience of the target group the marketer wants most to reach.

With the exception of those enterprises that look to engage the seniors' market, most businesses—from entertainment and leisure to consumer goods to cars and electronics to corporate and business services—get extremely nervous as their customer base ages. As the pressure to reach younger decisionmakers increases, campaign themes, hooks, and positioning statements that emphasize history and experience become less relevant. Thirtysomething CEOs and entrepreneurs who have turned their ideas into successful ventures may not be impressed by something someone else did a century ago. They are on the "fast track," and want those who market to them to understand that.

Similarly, members of the younger, more trend-conscious consumer market segment generally not only do not *care* if a company has been around for a hundred years, but may count that very point *against* the company, regarding the company's interest in its own history as a suggestion that it might be less concerned with the needs and preferences of today's market.

Increasingly, the use of the time-honored selling point of having been in business for years is dying off with these generations. In professions such as the entertainment and computer industries, where many senior executives as well as staff members only know the Kennedy Administration through the documentaries on A&E's *Biography*, longevity and its many implied virtues are less important than other attributes.

Marketers will be encouraged by the fact that, apart from a product being new, exciting, and hot, quality, value, and uniqueness are still the essentials that define products, services, companies, and brands.

Once, some sage might have declared that in order to build a reputation worth exploiting—a good track record—what one needed most was simply *time* (to make and correct mistakes, as well as to build on successes). Time allows a company or business an opportunity to serve, perform, and earn labels that look good in ads and press releases—strength, stability, accomplishment, respect, integrity—the basic ingredients that are commonly associated with a good reputation. Time is no longer the most important consideration in today's market.

It is significant that when the trade magazine *Advertising Age* named five companies "Marketers of the Century," some of the companies listed had been in existence for only a relatively small part of that century. Yet they had leaped ahead of literally tens of thousands of other companies that had enjoyed a very large head start. It's been a long time since anyone has uttered the phrase that seemed to say so much: *as GM goes, so goes the nation.*

For many years, General Motors was not only the world's leading automaker, but the largest publicly held company in the United States. Naturally, a move in GM stock moved the market. If GM sales were strong, that was good economic news for the many businesses that were dependent on a strong auto industry. Literally hundreds of other industries reported that their business was better when people were buying more cars.

As time went on, technology and the still-emerging Internet economy transfixed business, the markets, and much of public consciousness. General Motors remained (and still remains) a very important global player, but its reputation is no longer that of the key mover in all the land. Nor did Microsoft or America Online, newcomers that changed the way millions of people and companies live and do business, run away with the blue ribbon (this time).

Leading marketers include such companies as Procter & Gamble, McDonald's, Coca-Cola, Anheuser-Busch, and Nike. When considered in terms of reputation marketing, how do these five highly respected and enormously successful companies measure up? Perhaps the single most significant characteristic that all share is that each one is a model for what both large and small, both established and start-up companies, aspire to be.

Certainly everything is relative, and a small service company probably doesn't believe it will become Procter & Gamble. But a successful company's strategic approach to marketing its products, and leveraging its reputation to attract talent, investors, and more business, is worth studying and adapting on a scale that works elsewhere.

Advertising is a powerful component in the marketing mix, and it's usually the most costly. Few companies will come up to the line with the ad budget of Coca-Cola or McDonald's. And of course, in building and shaping a reputation, traditional mainstream advertising, such as TV, radio, magazines, newspapers, and outdoor displays, is much more important to some companies than it is to others. The key determinants in the process must be to know (1) who you are trying to reach; (2) what the most effective medium would be to reach this group; and (3) how your marketing budget could be best applied to points one and two.

That is the short explanation of the method that these "role model" companies use to reach their target audiences and to establish and exploit reputations that serve their interests. Each of the companies directs its marketing messages to specific demographic segments. Despite the seemingly broad appeal of their products or services, each company has chosen to narrow its targets—a good strategy in a highly crowded and competitive marketplace. Each company has a core constituency to whom certain characteristics may be more or less important. Its reputation, however, has enormous influence over purchase decisions.

Most companies position their products as being cost-competitive. But indications are that in virtually every instance in which people have chosen in favor of the companies named, they did so on the basis of quality, convenience, image, and overall reputation, rather than on price. That was not always the case. In the days when GM was king, the lower prices of GM vehicles were truly a factor in a customer's mind. Now, the sticker price is largely an illusion when it comes to deciding on a car, truck, or SUV. Auto companies make much of their rebate offers and great deals in which they "slash sticker prices," but the typical cost of add-ons and financing are more than enough to offset any highly touted discounts, and in today's market, most customers understand this. A person's choice of a car largely comes down to the car's image and reputation and how those things fit with the customer's perception of his or her own image, as reflected in the reputation of the car.

Let's look closely at the five companies that have managed their reputations so successfully. Some of their stories are brief, like the histories of the companies themselves. Advertisers have long believed that more people will read a brief, concise advertisement than will read a much longer ad. Maybe, again, the rule is to know your audience. A successful approach that can be described in relatively few words is not less of a success. Similarly, if the members of your public know relatively little about you, but what they know leaves them with a favorable opinion, you have created a good reputation that can serve your purposes as well as if they knew much more.

■ Procter & Gamble

Procter & Gamble has a reputation as a company that manufactures and markets quality products, even though the consumer's choice is rarely, if ever, based on his or her knowledge that the brand is from P&G. Although enormous advertising support, power over distribution, and control of shelf space are certainly huge factors, brands such as Tide, Crest, and Ivory are not chosen by consumers because they are identified as P&G products, but because each continues to maintain its individual identity and nurture its own reputation for quality in the marketplace. This is an important factor in an era when powerhouse brands are increasingly being sold or spun off.

It is unimaginable, for example, that Hershey's would sell the candy bar that bears its name to any other company. The Hershey Chocolate Company would be a much richer, but highly odd, entity in the aftermath. However, should circumstances demand that P&G sell its Crest toothpaste unit to a rival toothpaste manufacturer—or for that matter, to a bank or tobacco company—Crest would not be diluted in value because of its disassociation with P&G. Nor would P&G be a lesser company for having one less brand of toothpaste (albeit a megagiant) under its flag. The point is that both the company *and* its star division have currency in the marketplace. Unlike Hershey, which has branded itself and its product as inseparable, Crest and P&G each maintain a flexibility and mobility apart from the other.

Pringles potato chips are a P&G product that were introduced in 1968. They sputtered along for more than twenty years before finding a market niche and emerging as an important global brand. Marketers and Wall Street analysts recognize that P&G has so much power that it can afford such practices, where other companies cannot. In that sense, not only its size, but its reputation over more than a hundred years for commitment and stability, is what sustains it as a company.

Indeed, P&G's ability to survive wild fluctuations in the stock market and extremes in the marketplace has positioned it well. But its reputation is clearly not based solely on the fact of its survival, but just as much on its ability to market many products and keep them competitive as decades go by.

Tide laundry detergent, for example, continues to be one of the most recognizable products of all time, owing to its familiar logo and package. Yet, the core product has been dubbed "new and

FIGURE 3.1 **Tide**

The familiar Tide laundry detergent logo has gone beyond the box, bottle, or tub. After dozens of "new and improved" versions, the product sells as much on its reputation for quality and consistency as for the attributes themselves. (Copyright 2000 P&G Co.)

improved" enough times to make one wonder if the current product bears any resemblance at all to the original. No matter: it outsells its competition, not only year after year but generation after generation, and appears to be ageless.

A lesson in reputation marketing might be that, if a product is perceived to still be doing its job—changing when it needs to in order to remain environmentally friendly, high in quality, and safe but maintaining its familiar and recognizable presence—marketers should continue to support it with advertising and promotional strength.

Casebooks are thick with examples of brands that were market leaders but lost the support (and funding) of managers, who diverted resources to new products that proved to be little more than flavors of the month.

P&G continues to maintain its reputation as a company people trust. Despite years of uneven financial results, the marketplace continues to regard P&G's management as bright, visionary, attuned to the market, and although conservative, not afraid to take chances on innovative products or ventures. It is an example of a company with a carefully managed and protected reputation for stability without complacency.

Unlike many other well-established companies, P&G's reputation was built more on results than on press releases. It wisely took credit for its successes and acknowledged its missteps while establishing enough successful products and brands that it was able to define itself, rather than allowing others to define it.

Additionally, P&G has managed to avoid being saddled with the image of a stodgy old company that wants to talk more about its history, suggesting that perhaps its best days are behind it.

Tide, Crest, Pampers, Ivory soap, Pringles potato chips, Bounty paper products, Charmin tissues, and other P&G brands have successfully built their own individual reputations as cate-

FIGURE 3.2 Dryel

Procter & Gamble has survived competitive peaks and valleys in part because it remains competitive and contemporary. A relatively new product, Dryel fabric cleaner, presents an ad that appears to be selling fashion, sex appeal, and "attitude." It positions the company, more than a century old, as anything but stodgy. (Copyright 2000 P&G Co.)

gory leaders. They have the advantage of support from the P&G mother ship, yet remain independent of the P&G logo. This strategy permits individual successes and stumbles by each brand, without affecting either the corporate parent's reputation or that of other brands in the P&G stable. P&G promotes its individual products' strengths and unique selling points (with the considerable muscle of solid P&G funding) without linking them back to P&G.

Although P&G must show its investors a good bottom line, one division should not (and does not) have to see its reputation suffer because of sagging sales in another, resulting in huge cuts in its marketing budget. While this may seem to be an obvious observation on sensible business practices, as well as basic fairness to a good performer, it hasn't always worked that way.

Conglomerates diversify through acquisitions as a means of increasing overall corporate value and reducing market risk in volatile industries. Many companies then go on to address the issue of paying down their considerable debt from the acquisition by reducing the operating budgets (particularly advertising and marketing) of the individual companies. The result is a company that appears to be challenging itself to do more with less, presenting an overall image of a weakened company.

P&G appears to be too smart for that. It understands the value of maintaining the brand equity of each of its established units and simultaneously treating its own corporate identity as if it were a brand, as demanding of attention and protection as the products visible on store shelves. There have been several fine histories written of Procter & Gamble, and it is rightfully viewed as a model of a successful conglomerate. But when it comes to reputation marketing, P&G has wisely positioned its *products* and the groups that market them at the forefront, using research to help define the most market-friendly message for each. So far, it's worked.

■ McDonald's

McDonald's has a reputation around the world as the company that redefined both the fast-food and franchising industries through its efficiency, quality, superb ability to locate its units at profitable sites, and an astute sense of merchandising and promotion: key elements of successful marketing. All this with less than a half-century of experience under its corporate belt.

The company does not dwell on its corporate past (unless one counts the daily numbers on the driveway signs that report the updated numbers of billions of hamburgers sold). Instead, it looks anxiously at the future and makes creative efforts to protect and expand its franchise.

How did such a relatively young company achieve the reputation of a superstar, finding itself so well positioned in two categories (fast-food and franchising) that competitors regard it as both the industry standard *and* the one to beat? McDonald's did not invent the concept of fast food—there had been drive-in restaurants and sidewalk vendors for decades—but it redefined the concept so dramatically that it has become the first name that springs to mind when people think about fast food.

Few people would challenge the statement that McDonald's has produced some of the most memorable ads in the history of advertising, whether they featured the expensively acquired presence of a superstar athlete, a rock star, or just an array of ordinary people—from senior citizens to toddlers—who looked like the folks down the block. The classic McDonald's line "You deserve a break today" remained identified with the company, enhancing its reputation as a superior marketer, long after the ad campaign that introduced it had ended. Additionally, the phrase heard in millions of homes and offices each day, "We'll just stop and pick up McDonald's," vaulted the brand to the unique level of Xerox, Coke, and

Kleenex in that "to pick up McDonald's" became synonymous with getting fast food.

In its early days McDonald's displayed its "golden arches" trademark, but rarely referred to the symbol. The company's marketing emphasis was totally on building up the McDonald's name and reputation in each of its communities. The closest allusion to a secondary marketing note was the continually updated references on its signage to the millions (later billions) of hamburgers sold.

As its name became better known, McDonald's masterfully demonstrated its unique ability to co-opt the most generic of foods with such designations as "McRibs," "McChicken," "McNuggets" (for bite-size chicken pieces), and "McFlurry" for whipped ice-cream desserts. The true master stroke, of course, was the christening of the simple hamburger club sandwich (two hamburger patties between three pieces of bread) as a "Big Mac." It quickly became one of the most recognized meals in the world, even among a generation of people often criticized for its unfamiliarity with cultural touchstones.

Ronald McDonald, a circus-clown character created for TV commercials and on-site grand-opening appearances, soon turned serious. He became the symbol of the company's charities for children, as well as the namesake of Ronald McDonald House, a residence and support center for families of children who require hospital care far away from home.

The company successfully softened critics' charges that it was marketing seriously unhealthy products, high in fat and cholesterol, at a time when other restaurant chains were promoting a healthier menu. McDonald's introduced salads, grilled-chicken sandwiches, and a lower-fat "McLean" burger, but these items sold marginally or poorly in most locations. Rather than the new items, it was McDonald's high-profile involvement in charitable and community activities that created a bubble of goodwill around the company, one which nutritionists could not burst.

The company wisely did not attempt to dispute, debate, or out-shout its critics regarding their laboratory analysis of the nutritional deficiencies of McDonald's products. It simply offered alternatives to its regular favorites on the menu board, while announcing that it would use only recyclable paper products and quietly increasing its sponsorship of local and international charitable or goodwill programs.

The public's affection for McDonald's was also obvious in the way the company was quickly forgiven for its highly visible failures, such as the Arch Deluxe. This "adult" sandwich, like the several failed versions of steak sandwiches that came before it, attempted to entice parents to the place that has a reputation for being the undisputed first choice of teens and preteens, not their parents. The reason for this reputation was simple enough: McDonald's was mag-nificently positioned as a supremely *kid-friendly* restaurant. One does not install indoor playgrounds in thousands of locations and expect to attract a customer who is normally inclined to white table-cloths and candles on the tables.

Despite purchases of the family-oriented chains Boston Mar-ket, Donatos Pizza, and Chipotle Mexican Grill, it is unlikely that McDonald's will attempt to cross-manage these brands (there are obvious conflicts in the short-term with franchise agreements) and just as unlikely that the company can be all things to all people, since they're the choice of burger lovers of all ages. An interesting test, featuring bratwurst sandwiches and buffalo wings in selected mar-kets during football season, marked the entry of brand-name prod-ucts without the familiar (and expected) "Mc" label. The company seems to recognize that adults are more receptive to products that they know by name and that aren't perceived to be "for kids."

How much is that doggie in the window?

Just $1.99. 102 toys from Disney's *102 Dalmatians*. One in every Hamburger Happy Meal!

FIGURE 3.3 McDonald's

McDonald's reputation is firmly entrenched for its fast food, so this ad doesn't even mention food but focuses instead on its tie-in to a Disney film and product. It may not make kids hungry, but it keeps the company's aim squarely fixed on its core market and reminds the audience who McDonald's wants to reach. (Copyright 2000 McDonald's Corporation; Copyright 2000 Disney Enterprises, Inc. All rights reserved.)

The special McDonald's meal for children is the "Happy Meal," but what would appeal to their parents? Probably not a "Teeny Beanie Baby," a popular toy that came with the Happy Meals in a special promotion. Customers lined up around the block for the toy, almost dismissing the food as just the price one had to pay to get the toy. Salads, chicken, roast beef, and other "adult" items continue to fall short in both sales and the type of sizzle that has excited the market.

McDonald's is focused aggressively on using such promotions as traffic builders. The company even signed a ten-year right-of-first-refusal deal with the Walt Disney Company for product tie-ins with forthcoming Disney movies. Sales, special discounts, and premiums will help to bring in customers, but rarely keep customers coming back once the sale ends and the coupons are gone. Simply put, if customers only come for the two-for-the-price-of-one special or the *Star Wars* glass, they can't—and perhaps never will—be counted as *true* customers who will keep coming back. The company continues to experiment with a variety of new menu entries.

In terms of its reputation marketing, McDonald's knows the drill. Its logo is one of the most recognizable in the world, and it's a place kids love. Attempts to increase multigenerational participation in its dining rooms will probably succeed. Not because of premiums or even lower prices, but because the upcoming generations of parents, unlike parents of generations past, were raised on McDonald's meals. They'll very likely retain a positive opinion of the company and perhaps have a favorite meal as well.

Over the years, McDonald's has also come to be recognized as a highly litigious company. Like Disney and Mattel, it moves swiftly and aggressively whenever and wherever it believes its name, logo, or image is being infringed upon or compromised. Though it sometimes appears heavy-handed, McDonald's reputation as a kid-friendly, charitable, good corporate citizen so dominates public

opinion that it overshadows any miscalculations in judgment. The
public, its shareholders, and the market in general simply seem to
want to like McDonald's.

In mid-2000 the company unveiled a plan for a "makeover" that
will test video games at some locations and the addition of ethnic
items to some menus. Such innovations keep the business looking
fresh, but McDonald's and other companies have run into trouble
in the past when they departed from the formulas that made them
successful with their core markets. In McDonald's case, that's kids
and fast-food lovers. Hopefully the company will accept that it does
not have to be (or serve) all things to all people to remain the industry leader in what it does.

■ Coca-Cola

No one is ever surprised to find Coca-Cola wherever it appears—in
movie theaters, law offices, vending machines, or on a list of the
three most recognized logos in the world. (McDonald's and Marl-
boro are the other two.) So with all its corporate power and influence, how does Coke measure up when it comes to reputation
marketing, and how relevant is it as an example of a company others might emulate? Coke may be the giant at the top of the moun-
tain—an unrealistic height for most businesses—but an examination
of how the company built its reputation, and what it does to maintain and exploit it, will provide valuable insights for companies of
any size.

Coca-Cola has, from its earliest days, been protective of its
reputation. It became even more protective of its name as its success propelled it into a class by itself.

Much has been made of the "cola wars" in which Coke and its
chief rival, Pepsi-Cola, have been battling for supremacy for more

than a half-century. As the market leader, Coke is regarded by all as the one to beat.

Among the most memorable Pepsi campaign messages were claims that it was "the choice of the new generation" and "for those who think young." Both slogans implied, of course, that Coke was the choice of the *old* generation and, therefore, was for those who "think old." These observations were directed toward a culture largely obsessed with staying and feeling and acting *young*. The campaigns were good advertising and were well-received, but when the dust settled, Coke was still number one in market share.

The "Pepsi Challenge" bypassed the supermarket checkout aisles and took its case to the people in local parks, on beaches, and on sidewalks in downtown business centers. Pepsi would offer two paper cups of soda as a taste test and *dare* anyone to say, with a camera rolling, that they liked the taste of Coke better. Some did.

Although few people took the Pepsi Challenge seriously as market research, it did achieve Pepsi's objective of positioning itself as the irreverent, feisty contender for the crown. Again and again over the years, Pepsi would claim that it had gotten the better of Coke and was emerging as the people's choice. Pepsi's CEO even wrote a book called *The Other Guy Blinked: How Pepsi Won the Cola Wars*.

So despite all the battles, and Pepsi's claims of having achieved a knockout, why is Coke still the market leader by a wide margin?

The first reason is purely business. Coke is so far ahead in fountain sales to restaurants, bars, and other outlets where the product is not sold in bottles or cans that no competitor even comes close to its annual sales volume.

Secondly, the biggest challenge to Coke comes not from a small, independent company, but from Pepsi, another corporate monolith. Although Pepsi often attempts to portray itself as the lit-

tle guy in a David-and-Goliath scenario, Pepsi-Cola is actually perceived more as a giant throwing punches at another giant, who
might say "Ouch" now and then but never falls over.

Most importantly, Coca-Cola has taken great care in protecting its franchise, its image, and its reputation. It is a very high-profile
sponsor of concerts, awards programs, and many sports events, both
major and minor. The company identifies itself with excellence
through its sponsorship, from the Olympic Games to televised
awards programs.

Recalling a 1971 television commercial that featured a gathering of young people from all over the world on a hilltop, joining their
voices in song, writer Louise Kramer noted, "In one of the most
masterful marketing efforts of the twentieth century, Coca-Cola
Company managed to transform its soda into a brand that promises
to make the world a better place."

The song from that commercial, *I'd Like to Teach the World
to Sing (in Perfect Harmony)*, went on to become a multimillion-
selling hit record. It was played on thousands of radio stations each
day for months, and despite the removal of references to "buy(ing)
the world a Coke," the public sang along with it and thought of
Coca-Cola every time.

The lesson for marketers decades later is that, whether consciously or unconsciously, the public was aligning itself with the
product that wanted to teach the world to sing about peace and love,
rather than the product that was issuing "challenges" and implying
that its rival was the soft-drink choice of old people. That Coke has
retained its dominance appears to prove the point.

A corporate-image marketing program can create goodwill
through supporting local schools, sports, and community centers by
providing products and/or funding. The program can be adapted
and customized for use by large or small companies: locally, nation-
ally, or globally as budgets and market parameters dictate. And rep-

utations will be the better for it. A marketer's logo on the wall or screboad in the local school gym is every bit as powerful a message to an audience as the Coke logo is at the Olympic Games.

■ Anheuser-Busch

The history of Anheuser-Busch is one of hard work, vision, and the realization of the American dream: a German immigrant begins a brewery in the late 1800s; it becomes the United States' first nationwide brewing company in the 1950s; and achieves the status of market leader by 1957.

For people who like the companies they deal with to have a long history, Anheuser-Busch has a great story to tell. It has surpassed its modest beginnings and survived depressions, recessions, world wars, and a roller-coaster stock market.

But its reputation was not built on exploiting its longevity— that was merely put out there for the record. Some credit A-B's unshakable belief in the power of advertising, others credit its series of funny TV commercials over the years. Today, the company is one of the largest advertisers in the world.

But not every company looking for success and market share can become one of the country's largest advertisers. Let's consider, then, what else the company has accomplished: Busch Gardens in Florida and Virginia are popular tourist destinations for young and old alike, with the one in Florida holding its own in a state that's one of the most aggressively marketed vacation destinations in the world; the Grand Clydesdales, a majestic company-owned stable of show horses, are featured in virtually every televised parade during any holiday or celebration. They frequently appear in Budweiser commercials as well.

Perhaps more than anything else, A-B has carefully focused on its market and tries to give the people what they want, both in terms

FIGURE 3.4 Budweiser

Anheuser-Busch does a huge amount of quality advertising in all media for Budweiser and its other brands. In this print ad, however, the company focuses hard on its message "Be a designated driver and everybody wins!" It is a well-conceived pitch—a responsible maker of beer urging drinkers to behave responsibly. It could have come off as gratuitous and insincere as so many public service ads do, but Budweiser's agency strikes the right balance here and provides an example of why A-B is on the list of top marketers of the century. (Copyright 2000 Anheuser-Busch, Inc., Brewers of Budweiser.)

of product values and marketing messages. That could mean the rather odd—even by advertising standards—use of the comically lovable dog Spuds MacKenzie as a corporate spokesperson; ants; Lonnie the Lizard; or characters that parody current contemporary styles and expressions like "I love you, man."

Anheuser-Busch makes and sells beer and it has never appeared self-conscious about that fact, in the way that many tobacco companies have seemingly attempted to market their products while simultaneously trying to distance themselves from those very products. A-B's public face has consistently reflected a commitment to causes, such as the environment, and community, through grants and sponsorships. Its advertising and marketing sold beer, but the company's corporate positioning throughout its history has shown a dignified business. In times when its industry came under fire, this approach has served them well. The Busch family still has control of the company and is widely regarded as being well-connected politically. Many of its ads carried strong suggestions of patriotism, which has not hurt its reputation either.

■ Nike

Nike running shoes and sports apparel first appeared on the scene in the 1970s, and only registered an impact in the marketplace in the 1980s. It was the brilliant decision to sign basketball superstar Michael Jordan to an endorsement deal in 1985 and launch the enormously successful Air Jordan shoes that really catapulted Nike to its status as a superstar marketer.

Among the most successful marketers noted, Nike is the only one to position itself as having an "attitude." The late 1990s gave marketers a new definition of that term. It was not just a reflection of behavior, but a more obvious projection of independence—even defiance—that set a person (and a brand) apart from whatever constituted mainstream behavior. Members of Generation X (people mostly in their early twenties in the 1990s) embraced it as their own; "having an attitude" became for them what being a rebel had meant to their parents.

And riding the wave of this attitude was Nike.

Every generation looks for symbols to identify with—long hair, torn shirts or jeans, short skirts, button-down collars, head-bands, gold chains, bumper stickers—something that "makes a statement" about who they are and what they stand for. For a generation in search of itself, Nike offered a symbol and promoted it aggressively.

Running shoes as a symbol of rebellion and individuality? Nike sold them that way—and at a premium price. "Edgy TV commercials featuring Mr. Jordan focused on a whole new way to market footwear: linking sport, fashion, and a hip lifestyle," wrote Wayne Friedman in *Advertising Age*. "Revolutionary youth-targeted TV commercials gave Nike a clear, cool identity that has virtually defined sports apparel."

Mr. Friedman also noted, "Taking a commodity athletic shoe and turning it into a fashion statement took vision, edgy creative, and a once-in-a-lifetime presenter named Mike."

Going beyond shoes, Nike's line of sports clothing aimed for a similar nontraditional image. One ad, showing a young woman deep into a workout, carried the headline: "Just because you're a nice girl doesn't mean you can't have evil legs."

The headline was followed by the Nike logo and signature, with no copy. The ad was quirky, different, and typical of what would characterize the company's advertising for at least the next two decades.

Campaigns with lines and themes like "Just do it" and "Bo knows . . . " (the latter featuring sports star Bo Jackson, an addition to the Nike roster of celebrity endorsers), confused the "unhip." These campaigns expanded the Nike reputation for producing consistently cool, cutting-edge advertising. TV commercials directed by the equally edgy A-list film director Spike Lee attracted huge amounts of publicity and attention, and helped to enhance Nike's reputation as a maverick among leading brands. And the announcement that superstar golfer Tiger Woods had signed a Nike endorsement contract was almost met with a yawn. People would have been surprised if he had signed with anyone else.

As the new century began, Nike had grown from the upstart it had been only three decades earlier into a $10 billion company and a market leader. Still, it sought to preserve its outsider image.

Reebok, Adidas, and other competitors also positioned themselves as contemporary and stylish, and they did very well.

Nike, however, did better.

Its reputation is unique—that of the irreverent outsider who just happens to be the market leader. Nike has been able to accomplish this by having the foresight to sign some of the hottest names in professional sports, just as they stood at the threshold of superstardom. Nike persuaded creative "outlaw" directors and other unconventional talents to work for the company, giving them degrees of artistic freedom unusual in advertising. And Nike pledged that it would run what they produced, regardless of how quirky or unusual it might appear. The less the mainstream audience understood "what it meant," the more appealing it would be to the younger audiences Nike wanted to attract.

What lies ahead is the challenge of convincing the next generation that Nike is not so closely associated with a previous generation as to warrant rejection. The company does not have a long history to draw upon, and even to try marketing that history would run counter to the image it created—that of being on the cutting edge of style and product innovation. This is not a strategy that benefits from emphasizing its past successes. As with the teams and players of the various sports represented by Nike products, an illustrious history is impressive, but it is the score of the game you are playing now that counts.

Virtually every day, another company sets up shop with hopes of being the next Nike, McDonald's, Starbucks, or Microsoft—the superstars of marketing, which only a few decades ago set up shop with high hopes. . . .

Having a good reputation that includes decades (or centuries) of successful performances is a nice footnote. The most likely selling point, however, will continue to be the USP: the unique selling point, the key consideration that best sets you apart from competitors and makes you, or what you have, different or distinctive.

The difference in your product may be in the quality, pricing, distribution, value, or simply in the packaging. It may be that you are the brand associated with sports heroes like Michael Jordan or the sponsor of a children's charity campaign or leading the way in environmental protection. A distinctive product or service is a big help, but after that, it's all marketing. The reputation you create and maintain is the foundation, and its strength determines how high you are able to build.

SUMMARY OF CHAPTER THREE

- The length of time that a company has been in business is a selling point when it's used to imply that its longevity and survival of competitive challenges are good indications of quality and value.
- As the emphasis on reaching a younger market segment becomes more intense, a product, brand, or company's history and experience become less important selling points.

- Identify your target market carefully and sharpen your message to make clear what the value of your product or service is to them.

- If a product is perceived to still be doing its job, marketers should continue to support it with advertising and promotional strength, rather than introducing something new *just because it's new*.

- More important than how long a company has been around is what the company *has done* in that time in terms of innovation, quality, value, and service to customers and the community at large. Then it is time to describe the company's role in the market of today and tomorrow.

CHAPTER FOUR

Looking the Part

*Dressing for Success, for Failure,
or Just to Be Noticed*

**It's better to be looked over than
overlooked.**

—Mae West

There's a good chance that at some point, your mother mentioned to you the importance of making a good first impression. As is so often the case, your mother was correct. Despite philosophical disagreement about whether first impressions *should* be so important, they are. A first impression is the earliest step in creating and defining your reputation.

This is no less true when creating a marketing presence than when managing the rest of your life. People really *do* judge a book by its cover. Many fine books go unread because of a cover that is boring or off-putting, and many fine products fall flat because they *look* flat. Salespeople know they only have those first few seconds to "hook" a prospect, to capture his or her attention completely enough to continue on through the pitch and hopefully make it to the close.

This chapter will examine the concept of the *corporate identity*, which consists of components such as a name, look, logo, signature, corporate colors, and placement. Your name and look are the first messages you send to your market. Creating your reputation and establishing a continued presence build out from there.

Keep Things Simple

Think of creating your corporate identity as "dressing for success." When that concept was first advanced, some people scoffed at it, implying that it placed too great an emphasis on the superficial, on putting *style* over *substance*.

Nonsense. The very opposite is true. Anyone not placing importance on the look, sound, and overall impression a company makes is exhibiting arrogance, perhaps even disrespect for the market. If this seems to be an overstatement, it is not so by much. Marketers sometimes refer to their attempts to win acceptance in the marketplace as a "courtship," and most courtships begin with trying to make a good impression.

Think of your corporate identity as something like a dress code—defined, inflexible, and with an element of symbolism.

Companies with difficult or complex names invite misspellings and mispronunciation, two occurrences marketers should try to avoid. Since company names are often those of founders (sometimes the founder's daughter, as was the case with Wendy's and Sara Lee), or perhaps of complicated technical processes associated with the company's product, it may seem reasonable to you to go with that and simply expect your public to learn it. But have you considered that what seems reasonable *to you* may not seem reasonable to your target audience? After all, it is the *audience* you are supposed to be trying to impress. Keeping your identifiers simple and easy to write, say, and find in a directory goes a long way toward creating goodwill.

Corporate-identity programs typically impose restrictions on the use of the company name and logo, insisting that they must only be used as intended—not hyphenated, broken, or modified. This is reasonable and appropriate. Many companies, having invested heavily in establishing corporate colors, will require that when a logo or signature is reproduced, it is the designated PMS or corporate color. It is even understandable to insist that when a logo is used among other logos, a particular placement or position be adhered to and a size relationship of one logo to another be maintained. But businesses need the exposure that leads to greater awareness and acceptance. And when trying to gain that exposure, the fewer restrictions the better.

Yahoo! is one of the most successful Internet search engines. The company insists that the exclamation point that follows its name is a part of its legally registered name and should always be used. The public and the media generally regard this as anything from amusing (at best) to annoying (at worst). The fact that the name has no relationship to Internet search engines doesn't help either. The most frequent comment on it may be that it is "too cute by half."

Cute? Maybe. But does it help create goodwill or a good reputation for the company? Not that anyone can tell. In an ocean of search engines, Yahoo! was one of the more successful ones. Who can say if it would have been even *more* successful if it hadn't presented itself in a way many people felt was silly? In reputation terms, *silly* is not a positive word to describe a business that wants to be taken seriously.

Using Words as Pictures

Consider the power of certain words that immediately call up an image:

Playboy
The New Yorker
Malibu
Mustang
Secret
Virgin
Everest
Camelot
Cambridge
Riviera
Safari
Saturn
Alpine
Stingray
Sundance
Morningstar
Milky Way
Rembrandt
Suave
Polo

The twenty names on the list are, of course, those of well-known products. In reviewing the entries, did *Riviera* produce a mental image of a Buick? How about the French Riviera? Did *New Yorker* make you think of the sophisticated literary weekly magazine? Was the mention of the word *Polo* enough to conjure an image of the "gentlemen's game" of skill and horsemanship, a magazine, a fine aftershave or cologne, or a line of designer clothing by Ralph Lauren?

Whatever images each person attaches to the entries on the list is less important than the fact that some image comes to mind.

It is not likely that someone choosing a Milky Way candy bar will actually be moved to think of constellations and galaxies in a night sky. However, a product name that is synonymous with open, peaceful, starry skies is more likely to strike a positive note with consumers than, say, *Zagnut* or *GooGoo Cluster*, to mention two competing candy bars that have never quite set the marketplace on fire.

Quality, value, and image are essential elements in a strong marketing message. Starting out with a name that helps your cause is a good idea as well.

When Marketers Lose Their Way in Cyberspace

In the 1990s, as the "Internet explosion" took over Wall Street, having "dot-com" at the end of a company name was a useful way to distinguish it as being primarily a website or an Internet address. But before it ran out of gas, the dot-com craze that created a pinata of new businesses also launched a generation of "dot-com" companies that spent millions of dollars advertising and marketing themselves without ever telling the public what exactly it was that they did.

An issue of the hot technology magazine *Red Herring* listed more than 150 companies in its index. Less than a dozen of these companies were known to the general public. That means that the overwhelming number of companies were not (or not *yet*) well known; this is acceptable for a relatively young industry. But how much did their names tell us about who they were, what they stood for, who they wanted to reach, and what they offered? Consider:

Amgen

Appstream

Ashanti

Business.com

Buzzsaw.com

Digex

E-Sim

Flying Crocodile

Intira

Jamcracker

Janwal

Eprise

Throughout history, there have been stories of companies that languished in obscurity until they achieved breakthrough success and suddenly became well known, because they had the right product or service and marketed it well. And some of these companies came with odd-sounding names that fell well outside of the American/National/General mold, such as Smuckers and Orville Redenbacher. The conventional wisdom held that they shouldn't have been accepted by the public. Such success stories are both legendary and the exceptions to the rule.

A reputation is cumulative, taking into account how people come to regard an entity over time. For this reason, it is good business to begin shaping opinions as early as possible. Mistakes cannot be undone. Certainly people's opinions can be changed, but it is considerably easier for marketers to simply try to *avoid* as many missteps as possible, right from the start.

About.com is a large Internet company that has advertised on TV, radio, and in print media. It is, in fact, one of the better-known names in the dot-com category . . . and *still* it has not conveyed a clear sense of what it is or does to the millions of people who have seen its ads over a two-year period. This is not something investors like to hear.

Most marketers do not have the luxury of being able to go back and rename their company, but it makes sense to avoid compounding the problem by poorly marketing what the company has or does. If the name doesn't say what the company does, a positioning statement and advertising program should. Retailers who have been through a number of aggressive, competitive business cycles understand this, but it appears that many of the new, cutting-edge technology and service companies do not.

A clever name that makes everyone in the office congratulate themselves for "getting it" should not then compound the offense against the marketplace by launching its "insiders-only" label and expecting investors, analysts, customers, and the media to figure out what the company is about. Usually, they won't bother. This forces the clever people to have to look for other jobs sooner than expected.

For Eyes is an excellent name for an eyewear retailer. "For Eyes, specialists in quality eyewear" is a slogan that sells products.

This basic, commonsense approach seems so elementary as to not be worth mentioning. Yet, the year 2000's Super Bowl, one of the most expensive advertising venues of the year, carried dozens of thirty-second-long commercials for companies the public had not heard of before—or since. No one knew what the companies did.

A year later, the advertising industry was still talking about what had been an interesting, if somewhat embarrassing, episode in its history. After all, ad agencies were supposed to creatively and effectively generate awareness and recognition for their clients.

Instead, Super Bowl XXXV is remembered as a time when many agencies simply played "take the money and run." Companies wasted large amounts of their venture capital on self-indulgent exercises—minidramas, minisitcoms, and in some cases, just rock music and rapid-fire quick-cut images—that did not help to create a good reputation for themselves or their products (or in fact, any reputation at all). By the following year, most of the advertised entities no longer existed.

Basic Rules for Building a Reputation

How you look and what you do creates an image. Images, over time, create a reputation. Through your advertising, public relations, package design, delivery system, unique selling points, presentation, performance, and quality of service, you have positioned yourself in the marketplace.

Tell people who you are.

Tell them what you do.

Tell them why they should care.

A marketing effort is the time, place, and program that should be used to promote quality, cost, value, and your best and most unique characteristics—the features that set you apart from everyone else.

Make the public *want* to get a closer look at you, to know more about you.

There is a pretty basic reason why very attractive models work more often than the more average-looking models. The marketer who announces that he or she is going to use "real people" in ads or marketing campaigns probably remembers hearing the arguments about the importance of substance over style and how beauty is only skin-deep.

Nonsense.

First, there is no reason why you cannot, or *should* not, have both substance and style. Second, people can see "real people" anytime. The practice of using models who look like the people you want to reach is not as attention-getting or persuasive as using models who look the way the target audience *wants* to look. When people are being courted to buy a product or service, or to support an issue or a cause, the marketer's job is to make the experience memorable and pleasurable to the greatest extent possible.

If, as defined earlier, a reputation is the cumulative effect of images conveyed and impressions made over time, you should consider the "delivery mechanism" for those images. Not everyone reads magazines or newspapers. Some people never listen to a radio or surf the World Wide Web. It is important to know this, to know your audience and where your audience can be found. Let your "look" help distinguish you and make an impression. For example, if the idea is to stand out and be remembered, consider:

- News commentator George Will usually wears bow ties, especially when surrounded by fellow newsmen who will likely be wearing their red or green power ties.
- Writer Tom Wolfe long ago adopted a "signature" look, wearing only white suits.
- Congresswoman Bella Abzug was easily recognized by her trademark hats and became identified with them, particularly since she wore hats in situations where they were not normally seen.
- Managers and top salespeople for Mary Kay Cosmetics drove the company's very distinctive pink Cadillacs, and representatives of the bestselling brand of Scotch whisky Cutty Sark drove Cadillacs that were gold and green. Both were easily identifiable and became synonymous with the brands, while

the driver's obvious success was associated with the companies' products.

- Anything that has to do with UPS (trucks, uniforms, drop-off boxes) comes in a chocolate brown.

Second Impressions and Growing with Your Market

Since reputations are built over time, a marketer's relationship to his or her business or consumer market should be ongoing—not just a matter of conveying an image, making a good impression, making the sale, and moving on. The very idea of exploiting a reputation for marketing purposes suggests the desire of the marketer to create and maintain relationships over time.

Because your look is an important part of how people will know you, it is important to be aware of market sensitivities and to avoid offending anyone.

People who make up the younger market segments will someday be old, and since their tastes are likely to become more discriminating as they grow older, the marketers must either grow with them and hold their interests, or lose them. Again, the "take the money and run" approach is not good marketing.

Market to the Customer, Not the Company

Marketers must create a "comfort zone" for the public with advertising and other marketing messages. That, of course, starts with the presentation of a well-conceived overall look for a product, brand, or company. It is a balancing act for marketers to come up with a

name, a look, and a presence—the total combination of elements—
that will clearly reflect the subject's uniqueness and yet present it in
a way that allows the market to respond favorably on its own terms.

Too often, as companies become insulated from their public,
they tend to think *internally*, designing and presenting their packaging and their messages in a way that reflects more what the *company* wants than what the *market* wants. It is critical that marketers
keep the company focused on the fact that it is the market that gets
to decide what succeeds, not the company.

Clearly, there are examples of companies that spend considerable time and money to "precondition" the market, so that the public decides that it needs or wants what is being offered. But in a time
when response and success are increasingly registered and meas-
ured in shorter intervals, few companies have the luxury of time, or
the patience, or the budget to work such a strategy. That brings the
focus back to knowing the market and giving it what it wants (based
on current perceptions)—and doing so in the least exclusionist or
offensive way.

Companies who pitch to specific demographic groups are
increasingly operating on perceptions—often erroneous perceptions—of what is wanted, rather than taking the pulse of the market with targeted research. Ads for younger audiences that show
young models in "wacky" clothes, wild hair, a deliberately "oddball"
look, and multiple piercings in very visible places (nose, lips, eye-
brows) are representations of a young person as perceived by an
advertising agency. Many young people, seeing such a representa-
tion, resent it or dismiss it. This is less a reflection of a generation
gap than a failure of the company, marketer, or agency to study the
market and create the consumer comfort zone to support the marketing message.

Some marketers believe presenting imagery that shows
extremes in order to make a point is a way of bonding with an audi-

ence. But they fail to consider the composition of the *total* audience. There are many people of every age and any number of lifestyles who do not look like (or respond to) extreme characterizations. These audience members see such depictions as examples of marketers (1) not knowing them and (2) attempting to overtly manipulate them with imagery that insults their intelligence. They tend to view such moves as pandering, if they take the time to view them at all.

Seniors, baby boomers, members of Generation X, and a number of identifiable ethnic groups, to name a few examples, are known to base their choices on a perception that the marketer or company "speaks" to them. The product or company name, packaging, position statement, and the attempted imagery are the "speakers."

Again—all too often—corporate egos create a look or a name and report that it "tests well." A bit of probing reveals that the testing was done among those persons present in the executive suite when the boss asked how many people agreed with the choice he just made. This procedure is not regarded in test-evaluation circles as state-of-the-art market research.

An example of this might be the coffee marketed under the brand name Millstone. Following the phenomenal success of Starbucks Coffee (in the company's coffee shops around the world and with a supermarket version of its product), others have attempted to grab a piece of this new market. Categorized as "designer coffees," "gourmet coffees," or "yuppie coffees," Brother's Gourmet Coffee, Gloria Jean's Coffee Beans, and Seattle's Best Coffee have all taken their shots at getting a piece of the, uh, bean. Maxwell House, Hills Brothers, and Folgers added premium-blend lines in new upscale packaging. But perhaps the most heavily promoted new entry in this category is Millstone.

The brand's packaging, positioning, and advertising are clearly aimed at appealing to the Starbucks customer. The coffee might very well have a great price, quality, and flavor, but its name suggests that

FIGURE 4.1 Millstone Coffee

Millstone Coffee is a young brand that must establish its reputation. This richly drawn ad presents the product as if it were already established and not a Starbucks wannabe. The beautiful couple in the ad are dancing or embracing in a vineyard, over the word Seductive—*inspiring images of wine and romance. They are not drinking coffee and that's what the ad wants the reader to do. For the company to earn a reputation as a purveyor of fine coffee, it needs to make the audience "think coffee." (Copyright 2001 Millstone Coffee, Inc.)*

either no research or testing was done at all or that the company has no interest in attracting discerning customers, those who attach any importance whatsoever to a product's name. True, a millstone is a combination stone used in grinding (as in a mill), but a millstone is also *a heavy emotional or financial burden*—as in the expression "a millstone around one's neck." It is curious why anyone thought this would be a good name for a high-end brand of coffee. If this is careful image marketing, why is the image offered to much of the audience so depressing?

Although an overwhelming number of Starbucks customers may not know that the product's name comes from a character in *Moby Dick*, Starbucks is not a word or a name its target market would call "a downer." A good guess might be that the name *Millstone* was chosen because somebody liked how it sounded, and simply didn't do any homework to determine if even a small percentage of the market would be turned off by it. Is this a big deal? Only to marketers who know the dollar value of even 1 percent of a multi-billion-dollar market. To advance a positive image and create a positive reputation, don't start with a negative.

Looking Serious

A company's look and name should not simply be a reflection of the senior management's personal tastes. Nor should it be based on legends or folklore.

For years, banks and financial-service companies avoided using the color red in logos, signatures, or marketing materials because legend held that it left a "subliminal" suggestion of red ink—synonymous with losses, negative balances, and financial disaster. Green, the color of money, and blue, suggestive of calmness and serenity, were the colors of choice.

Nonsense.

First, on the matter of subliminal suggestion (planting an idea that is not noticed consciously, but is registered *unconsciously* in someone's mind and therefore, supposedly, has a significantly greater influence): all that has ever been proven beyond a doubt is that the theory helped one individual sell thousands of copies of three separate books and a lot of tickets to his lectures. Subliminal suggestion, if indeed it exists at all, is not some secret method for successfully creating an awareness, loyalty, or desire to buy on the part of the consumer. Well-managed banks with a red-letter logo have enjoyed as much success as well-managed banks with blue or green logos. White lettering is not suggestive of "white knights" or "white hats" (therefore, the *good guys*) any more than black type in a logo or signature leaves a bad impression because it signifies darkness or evil.

The look should fit the product or service, and help create an image that will add to a reputation. Research has told us that the market responds more favorably to certain colors and typefaces in specific situations. Funeral chapels should not have red signs or logos that suggest anything other than seriousness, or even solemnity. Amusement parks should not have black lettering on a white background, which could remind visitors of a law office or a government agency. This is common sense. Banks and hospitals shouldn't have signs with flames shooting through the lettering; high-end, elegant clothes should not have labels that look like a random assembling of letters in a ransom note.

If you have a look or a familiar logo that has become identified with you in a positive way and it seems to be working for you— sharpen it, frame it, and keep it. It gives you a reputation for consistency, stability, and durability.

If you're trying to decide on a look or a logo, a good shortcut is to look at what your competitors are using and *how* they're using it (for example, in media, packaging, or marketing materials). Analyze which aspects of the competitors' ideas work and which do not—and why. Sometimes a good ad will be scratched and labeled a bad ad, or a good package designer will be blamed for poor sales, when the problem was really distribution or shelf placement.

In the 2000 presidential election, Al Gore was reported to have hired the feminist writer Naomi Wolf, an image consultant, who advised him to wear brown suits and darker-colored shirts to create a look of independence and confidence—an "alpha male" look. What it created was months of embarrassment for the candidate to live down. For more than twenty-five years in public life, the candidate had been criticized for many things, but none of them had to do with his wardrobe. This superficial and cosmetic adjustment worked *against* the candidate, suggesting that even he thought the substance of his message was less important than its packaging.

Of course, both substance and packaging are important. But it can never appear as though a makeover is being adopted to cover a lack of substance or quality. Particularly given something as high-stakes as presidential politics, the emphasis needed to be on the packaging of the candidate's *message*, not the candidate's body. Improvements in wardrobe, hairstyles, makeup, and demeanor (read: stiffness with an air of pomposity) should be phased in carefully and gradually, with subtlety, not so suddenly as to call special attention to the changes. When a feature story is about a candidate's (or a corporate CEO's) new wardrobe, hairstyle, latest makeover, or "look" in general, and not about his or her ability to lead an organization or position on the issues, the candidate (or CEO) has a major problem.

Advertising and public relations exist to promote and raise the profile of a subject, but they should never become the subject themselves. Similarly, makeovers in product packaging, or an entirely new corporate-identity program, should be based on careful reasoning and necessity—utilized to enhance an image and bolster a reputation. Prematurely "freshening up" the look of an established company or product, or one that is still in its market-building phase, can convey a message that the company is badly in need of such freshening up and is therefore in trouble. To create a reputation of stability, it's necessary to appear stable. This aim is not helped by an inconsistent look.

The company has a product or service, and that product or service presumably has quality and value to a constituency. Although some companies and their agencies really do believe that any publicity is good publicity (and that a spot on the evening news will help advance the company's reputation), it's simply *not true*.

In instances where internal news is treated as a major business story, it's because marketing people are publicly exercising their corporate egos and asking to be given credit for their efforts. It *is* nice to be recognized for one's work, but a media event built around the approval of a budget, a new advertising campaign, or some other such "inside" piece of business does little or nothing to advance a company. It will neither promote an image nor add substance to a reputation, based on the quality of what the company offers the marketplace.

A company's new logo is *not* news. It does not provide anything of value to customers or stockholders.

When brands lose market share or appear to be going stale, very often the problem can be traced to a cutback in advertising or marketing activities. Companies redirect their energies (and budgets) to launching and establishing new brands or brand extensions. Although competition may remain strong, marketing efforts do not. A brand's decline is a reflection of such cutbacks and lack of support, more than most other market factors.

Present Marketing Images, Not Just Pictures

If the job is about marketing, focus on marketing. Publicists who represent entertainment-industry clients should generate publicity for their client's latest project: in the case of a film, what it's about; a TV program, why it's worth seeing; a recording or concert, why people should want to hear it. Publicists for corporations should promote whatever advances the image and reputation of the company or product and impresses the company's stockholders and the public. There seems to be a growing tendency to showcase everyone from actors and dancers to real-estate moguls and press lords as "people," releasing photos to the media of these individuals getting in and out of cars, entering and leaving restaurants, or walking through airports. The excuse for a news angle is often the revelation that these individuals are involved in new multimillion-dollar projects. But once the flashbulbs have stopped popping, the public will digest this information and realize that a person getting into a car is not actually news.

Just as distinctions should be made between a *press* release and a *news* release (both should offer information, only one need have actual *news*), marketers must understand that reputations are enhanced by offering substantive information rather than fluff.

A corporate look can be promoted through its presence in the relevant material (ads, brochures, or signs). Focusing on how long the new look was in development, what it cost, and why it is necessary diminishes the importance of the company's actual place in the market.

The image your name conveys, and its potential benefit to your reputation, is a lesson that appears to be lost on telephone companies. Examples of this are easy to find:

- When the U.S. government ordered the breakup of the phone-company monopoly, Illinois Bell ran an expansive ad campaign saying that it asked customers what they wanted in a phone company and the company's response was to change its name to "Ameritech."

  Is that *really* what the customers said they wanted? What about mentioning the cost savings, value, convenience, or quality of service with a tag like "And now we're known as Ameritech!"?

- In 2000, Bell Atlantic Corporation and GTE Corporation, two giants of the telecommunications industry with reputations to match, merged to create Verizon Communications. The new entity was launched with a cartoonish, multimillion-dollar ad campaign that took no notice of important points like the predecessor companies' powerful histories in their industry, just who would benefit from the merger, how anyone would benefit from the merger, or how the merger might improve service or save money. Verizon looked like one of the thousand dot-coms dotting the business section of the newspaper. Historically, phone companies have had poor reputations as uncaring monopolies, according to both the corporate sector and the public. Creating ads with messages that are irrelevant will do nothing to alter those reputations.

- Ameritech and Verizon are positioned to register a huge impact. They have the budgets and machinery to control the conversation in their industry. Their names have (or will become) known to their constituents, in large part because they appear on customers' bills every month. But the full range of what these two companies have to offer will not be readily known to those same customers as long as their marketers continue to implement corporate-identity programs that appear to be aimed only at pleasing the folks in the front office of their respective companies.

- Bell Atlantic and GTE, for better or for worse, had reputations that suggested credibility, stability, authority, service, and performance. The name, look, logo, ad campaign, and positioning of Verizon offer a new name that, although intending to suggest a futuristic technology company, has no history and no obvious links to the separate powers that created it. Basically, it starts at ground zero. It has resources and market access that other start-ups don't have, but its lack of a clear respect for its parentage makes a subtle statement to the market that whatever was identified with the former companies should not be assumed of Verizon. It may well become a great company, but it has begun by going at it the hard way.

In an era when we have not only Fridays, but casual *everydays* in the workplace, the old concept of dressing for success—with its power ties and executive-look accessories—now seems quaint. But that concept was not about individuals achieving the *GQ* look; it was about presenting an image of confidence, accomplishment, and predictability in order to create a customer "comfort zone."

The company version of the dress-for-success concept follows the same course:

- Know your market—what it wants and what it will accept.
- Choose an identifier that suggests a positive image and helps to convey who you are and/or what you do (as opposed to choosing an acronym or clever word from a seventeenth-century poem).

- Adopt a signature color that is pleasing to the eye and versatile in its application (such as the UPS chocolate color, which can be identified from a block away on shirts, caps, jackets, and trucks).
- Adopt a graphic presentation that reflects the image you have or hope to achieve. (High-tech companies don't use Old English, and a food company probably wouldn't use a high-tech look; instead, they would try to convey warmth and approachability through their graphic presentation.)
- Try to achieve a look that is distinct from that of competitors, but fits well within the perceived imagery of your industry or market niche (a signature in lowercase letters or letters with drop-shadows or all-bold caps; a unique package shape that still maintains industry consistency, such as the distinctively shaped bottles of Coca-Cola or the delicate green bottles of Perrier; the easily identifiable blue boxes and bags of Tiffany).
- Market yourself.

The last bullet point is not a joke. Logos, names, and distinctive packaging become familiar through their consistent and repeated exposure to their target market. Bring your look and your message to your public. Don't expect them to come looking for you.

Listen to the Market, Talk to the Market, Show Yourself

Following are five simple points to remember when bringing your message to your public:

- Advertise. Reputations are built by maintaining a steady, visible presence and by putting information about you in front of your public. If you wait for the market to come to you and ask about your offering, it's unlikely that you will become known to anyone except your immediate family.
- Let your corporate identity tell people who you are with a distinctive name and look. Logos as symbols of your company (instead of its name) are attractive, but meaningless if your public doesn't know you well enough to recognize your logo.
- Be direct. So often, marketers will try so hard to be clever by presenting a loud graphic with garish colors or complicated multifold ads and mailers, but will make the audience *work* to find the actual offer, or even the product.
- Tell your public who you are and what you do . . . again. The more frequently you tell them, the greater the chance you will become better known for what you do. A *better-known* company is often thought to be a *better company*, if only because it is better-known.
- A simple statement of your product's value and its potential benefits to the consumer, followed by your logo and signature, offers the steak and the sizzle, the style and the substance, the image that evolves into reputation. This approach is vastly more effective than the corporate ad or presentation that challenges the audience to find its purpose.

SUMMARY OF CHAPTER FOUR

- A name, a look, and a corporate-identity program should convey an image of what a brand, company, or product is, does, or has to offer.

- If a name doesn't say what the product or service is or does, a positioning statement and ad program should.
- People who are being asked to buy a product or support a cause should find the experience as memorable or pleasurable as a marketer can make it.
- A product's packaging can be distinctive regardless of whether it is understated, flamboyant, or anywhere in between.
- While being distinctive, be aware of the sensitivities of those people you are trying to impress. Don't offend.
- Create a "comfort zone" for your public while they are considering your advertising or marketing message.
- It is the people who make up your market who will decide whether or not you succeed, often simply because of your reputation. Try to give them what they want rather than what you want them to have, and you increase your probability of succeeding.

CHAPTER FIVE

Putting Your Reputation on the Line—*Online*

Reputation Marketing in the Internet Age

The unleashed power of the atom has changed everything save our modes of thinking, and we thus drift toward unparalleled catastrophe.

—Albert Einstein

In the late 1990s, after a quarter-century of limited use by university researchers and the military, the Internet emerged into the limelight to quickly become the darling of marketers. It was immediately labeled "new media," but it was so much more. Alas, by the year 2000, the bloom was off the rose; even some Internet boosters were downplaying its role in the marketing mix.

All the hype and great expectations aside, the Internet does offer highly viable possibilities. As with so many other aspects of marketing, however, it is first necessary to agree on what it is and what it is not.

Is the Internet another medium like television, radio, direct
mail, outdoor and print, or is it an entirely new instrument of education, the delivery system for "distance learning"? Should establishing a presence on the Internet be compared to opening a new
territory or location—a new "showplace"—in what may very well be
the largest mall and library complex ever devised? And in terms of
reputation marketing, is the Internet a useful tool, or the twenty-
first-century equivalent of a private club whose only members are
an eccentric community of techies?

The answer is that the Internet is not the end-all and be-all for
marketers, but it can indeed provide something for everyone.

As a medium, the Internet is unique. It affords a number of
possibilities: your website could be an interactive, highly customized
catalog; a repository of ads; a personal computer–driven online
home-shopping channel; a network of libraries; a meeting place; a
magazine; a picture show; a concert hall; or a department store.

But before either a new company hoping to make its mark or
a business with an established reputation sets about creating its
"Internet presence," it should have clear expectations for the result.

For a few years at the end of the twentieth century, anything
with a name ending in "dot-com" was considered hot, but by 2001
that same dot-com suffix had all the weight of a 1-800 number.
Indeed, the reputation of the Internet had suffered a devastating
blow. Thousands of overvalued Internet stocks, which had soared
on hopes of "what might have been," failed to show a profit and disappeared once their initial venture capital dried up.

Marketers need to learn from this experience that the failure
was not that of the Internet, but of the *companies*, who treated their
very presence online as justification for their future success. Every
lesson that marketers had learned up to that period seemed to have
been ignored, as if it did not apply in this case.

Big mistake. The World Wide Web is still alive and well, and despite the black eye it received from its misuse by greedy "new media" child geniuses, still offers a superhighway to opportunity.

Truly definitive research is still not available regarding the effectiveness of advertising and marketing a company's presence on the Internet relative to other media. But *advertising* that you're on the Internet in print ads, TV commercials, mailings, and posters, in places where you want to be and where your constituency will appreciate seeing you, will very likely enhance both your reputation and your market position.

Your Reputation Can Be Shaped by the Company You Keep

Media entities frequently exploit information about who their advertisers are, or who or what will be featured on their next program or in their next issue. In terms of your own image and the reputation you want, a good strategy is to exploit the fact that you are an advertiser and/or the subject of a story in a medium such as *National Geographic*, *The Oprah Winfrey Show*, MTV, or Comedy Central. In other words, go where your audience is so that they can see or hear your message, but more importantly, market and merchandise the fact that you are there.

It sends a strong message to a particular audience and demographic group when your ad or press release appears in the *Wall Street Journal* or *Forbes* or the *Weekly Standard*, three publications recognized for reaching conservative, upscale readers. (*The New Yorker* and the *Atlantic Monthly*, on the other hand, tend to attract upscale readers who are not necessarily conservative.) Readers accept the bond that is created when a company advertises in media that support social, economic, cultural, or political positions they themselves support.

Rolling Stone, People, Vanity Fair, Architectural Digest, Savvy, Details, and *Walt Disney Adventures* each have a clearly defined image and a clearly defined constituency. Content aside, the very *presence* of an ad in any one of these magazines sends its audience a message about how the advertiser would like to be regarded by its readers.

Advertisers who canceled their commercial spots on the often-controversial radio programs of Howard Stern, Rush Limbaugh, or "Dr. Laura" sent a clear message about what they thought of these hosts and their programs. These are perhaps among the more dramatic examples of how a reputation influences a media buy. Advertisers on these three programs are not only buying rating points and audience/market share, they are buying an *identification*—with the programs, their outspoken hosts, and their clearly defined points of view. To aggressively publicize the *cancellation* of ads on these programs is to attempt to distance an advertiser from the controversial programs, as blatantly as the original ad purchases had sought to identify with them. Perhaps more subtly, it also registers public disapproval. Such actions very directly define the reputation of the advertiser.

No single medium can be shown to have the edge over another until the proper profile of the target market segment is created. Once the profile is created, if magazines are shown to be a good advertising or marketing choice, the advertiser won't buy space in every magazine on the market, but instead will attempt to buy wisely and cost-effectively.

The publication, program, or website that reaches the audience you want to reach is important to your marketing mix not only for its ability to reach that audience, but *for the identification it provides you* with that media buy and audience. It is increasingly common for companies to issue press releases announcing that they have made a major advertising buy on a particular program, network, or website, as a way of identifying themselves with that property.

Finding Your Way on the Internet Superhighway

Many businesses, retailers, service providers, or catalog businesses create websites because they fear their reputations might suffer if they *don't* have an Internet presence, much the way ad-sales reps will tell potential advertisers that if their company doesn't advertise in a certain issue, it will be conspicuous in its absence.

Many others feel exactly the *opposite* and will never "do business with a computer," preferring personal contact and personal service. It is important for the marketer to know what percentage of his or her market falls on which side of this important preference issue.

Vince Gelormine, an Internet software and search-engine developer, notes, "Putting your information on the Internet is the easy part. It's a straightforward technical issue. The real tough part is getting to the right audience and getting them to visit your site."

Thousands of new businesses, and literally millions of web pages, constitute a new marketplace—much like a newly discovered planet. The scramble continues to find ways to tap this new market and use it both efficiently and profitably. The question asked most frequently is: since the public now has access to so much content on the Internet, will they be willing to pay for it? The answer is that most likely, users will be willing to pay. What is not known is *when*.

As with any new industry, many companies tried and failed (for every Amazon.com or e-trade.com, there would be thousands of failures), yet enough succeeded to keep alive the hope that there was still gold in the hills of cyberspace. It is noteworthy that Amazon, while still struggling, is regarded as one of the Internet's few real successes.

Several twenty-four-hour cable news channels and dozens of new publications have partnered with the new technology and actively promote it, often creating an exaggerated picture of its efficiency, maturity, and levels of public acceptance.

"Check out our website" is now the mantra of so many businesses that virtually every product, service, brand, and merchant has accepted the "necessity" of having a website too. In fact, that is not necessarily the case. To some users and site operators, the World Wide Web is a place to go for information. It is a directory, an encyclopedia, or a portfolio. It is "directory assistance" and the department-store window rolled into one. To others, the Web is a marketplace where buyers and sellers can meet to view and sample what is being offered.

"Cookies" planted on websites collect data on their visitors with an aim toward producing market research, building databases, or simply assembling E-mail lists to sell.

Millions of websites have become desktop malls for retailers, manufacturers, publishers, producers, service providers, dealers, marketers, fund-raisers, and pornographers.

A Well-Known Name Is Not Enough in Cyberspace

The rush to advertise online created yet another phenomenon: the often-bumpy—yet theoretically level—playing field, in which start-up companies frequently embarrassed old, established, successful companies. This gave credibility to claims of the Internet as the marketplace of the future. Online, the old, established brands had no real edge.

The premise that brand names had equity in the marketplace and could be used to great advantage was being challenged. The hottest names in Internet retailing were not Sears or K Mart, but e-Toys and Priceline.com. Market reports were headlined with news of major online failures by some of the best-known brands in the world, such as Levi Strauss and Mattel.

Shouldn't the better-known companies have prevailed? Didn't their worldwide reputations count for *anything* in cyberspace?

In many cases, no.

However, it also became clear that these companies did not always market their reputations to their greatest advantage. Instead, they arrogantly assumed that the presence of their names on websites would be enough to insure success.

Research indicates that companies or brands with an already-substantial catalog business should do well on the Internet. Their customers have already indicated a willingness—even a preference—to shop by phone or mail, making their choices and decisions from printed pictures and text descriptions. For the segment of this group that enjoys using personal computers, the website becomes an electronic edition of the catalog, direct-mail offer, or yellow-pages listing.

It is extremely important to note, however, that catalogs and direct-mail presentations arrive at home, work, or a waiting room unsolicited (although often beautifully presented). The recipient can passively take in the impressions that are offered. Websites, on the other hand, must be sought out by the user/potential consumer. This critical point totally changes the landscape: the printed catalog comes to you; the electronic catalog requires that you come to it. This underscores the case for using traditional media to promote a website, much the way radio and TV spots urge an audience to "look for our ad in this weekend's newspaper," or to "watch your mail for our special offer."

In the case of businesses where customers are accustomed to handling, trying, tasting, or smelling the merchandise, or being strongly influenced by packaging, displays, or showroom ambiance, it cannot be assumed that a website will have the same impact. An environment that removes the "hands-on" factor changes the dynamics between buyer and seller.

Levi Strauss spent years preconditioning its customers to try on their brand of jeans, and experience how they looked and fit, *before* making a purchase. Using a website to promote the brand was a viable idea for doing things like introducing new styles or features, or promoting special offers or coupons, as incentives to visit retailers that featured the brand. The jeans were a hard sell online to the established market, which still wanted to try on the product before buying it. Levi's website failed because it did not make use of the information it had about what its established customers wanted *and* what potential future customers wanted, in either a website or a pair of jeans. The website's failure was widely noted in the media and had a serious negative impact on the company's reputation.

Why do some marketers and manufacturers do well using the Internet in their marketing efforts?

Their market is either predisposed to shopping online, preconditioned to shop by direct-mail solicitations and catalogs, or both.

Lands' End, Victoria's Secret, and J. Crew are companies that have built their businesses and their reputations largely by displaying their offerings in beautifully photographed and thoughtfully presented catalog pages. Their websites serve as electronic editions of their catalogs for the particular market segments that prefer to view merchandise via this medium. The companies did not stop printing and mailing paper catalogs when they created their websites, but they *did* create incentives for current and future customers to put down the print edition and check online. There were frequently updated sale items or special promotions for online customers only. In the case of Victoria's Secret, there were online fashion shows. Traditionally successful media were used to give customers both a reason and an incentive to check the online catalog.

Ease and Convenience Are Still Important—Even Online

Most Internet customers understand that they have to wait for their merchandise to be delivered. They also realize that once it is received, if they should choose to return it for any reason whatsoever (very often a qualifier that contributes mightily to a business's reputation) or want to exchange the merchandise, a trip is required to a local post office or other shipper, and still another waiting period will elapse before the transaction can be called complete.

It should be noted that some companies use the Internet's point-and-click method as a selling point to suggest speed in ordering, but speed of *delivery* is what really counts with the customer; and that is up to the sender. Often, "faster-than-normal" service means an extra fee.

Be careful of these claims. Selling "fast service" by advocating the click of a mouse instead of a trip to the mall can backfire if the transaction drags on for days because of the process of shipping, exchanges, and returns. As annoying as a return visit to a store can be, it is nonetheless an option with which people are familiar. How such situations are handled in the online world has a lot to do with how the company is regarded. For example, books purchased at

BarnesandNoble.com initially could not be returned or exchanged at any of the book chain's stores. This upset a large number of customers, and by the time the situation was corrected, damage to the company's reputation was already done.

Expectations Must Be Realistic

Mattel's initial Internet experience was not positive. One of the largest and most successful toymakers in the world publicly revealed its disappointment (and dismissed its CEO) over its inability to create a viable Internet presence. Some observers wondered if the company's poor showing reflected a lack of clarity in what it expected of the medium. Like Levi's in an earlier example, Mattel is a successful manufacturer that does not sell its product directly to the public. Instead, it goes through toy stores and other retailers.

Mattel's online efforts might have gone better if the company had used its website as a promotional and support mechanism, helping to drive business into real-life stores and introducing brand extensions, such as the seemingly endless array of BARBIE doll products.

An ideal Mattel website would cross-promote the various lines of BARBIE merchandise. The packaging of the hundreds of BARBIE items could urge customers to "visit our website for special offers." An entire catalog of BARBIE and other Mattel merchandise could be displayed and updated regularly. Announcements could be made of special discounts that are *available* only to website visitors, but *redeemable* only at participating retail stores.

Catalogs, newsletters, magazines, and billboards are ideal media for websites to emulate. But when a site tries to be a chat room, catalog, customer-service department, and retailer all at the same time—when the brand is not primarily known to be *any* of these—it should not come as a major shock if across-the-board success does not follow.

Mattel is a manufacturer of toys and also has highly successful licensing deals that include cosmetics, TV shows, videos, music, books, and much more. The company's greatest successes have come from remaining in its own business and "partnering" with other competent firms that are experts in their fields when moving into another business. It is doubtful that a successful toymaker like Mattel would have thought of sacking its CEO if, for instance, a real-estate subdivision in which the company had invested had failed. Companies invest in things that are not sure winners all the time. But in this instance, the headlines every day had proclaimed the Internet the sensation of the business world, and Mattel's board of directors obviously wanted to be a part of it.

Mattel has the reputation of an industry leader. From this position, it could have used its website to create a club for its young customers, systematically engaging them to be loyal to the brand (as Disney has done so successfully). It could have been a "members-only" site, offering exclusive features that related to favorite toys and characters. Or it simply could have offered an electronic catalog of its products or an extension of its Saturday-morning cartoons. Mattel didn't seem to know what its website was to do, present, or be, only that the company should have a big Internet presence. And business is about specifics.

Mattel's experience online was a disappointment in part because its objective was not clearly to educate or entertain, but to promote—and without a clear sense of what the Internet audience was looking for. The company's Internet experience was not a quick success, though it might have done better over time. Mattel, despite its track record of hugely successful products and ventures, believed it had taken an embarrassing, high-profile hit and was not pleased.

Overall, the toymaker has maintained a relatively good reputation through the years. Staying focused on its true business and not overreaching will help it maintain that reputation.

Walt Disney is said to have required everything that came out of his company—whether it was a toy, film, book, TV program, or game—to educate and entertain. This philosophy added to Disney's reputation as the preeminent marketer of family entertainment, with expansive lines of merchandise created around each program or character. Disney is not simply viewed as a film company or a toy company, although both divisions are among the top names in those industries. The company's franchise, its name, and its reputation are carefully managed so that Disney stands for excellence, however it is represented. That philosophy is carried over to the company's website. Each time the site is accessed, the Disney reputation is reinforced through the family images, games, and promotions packaged as entertainment. Few have ever done it better.

Don't Wait for the Market to Come to You

For generations, marketers have carefully analyzed the impact and commercial viability of television, radio, print, and outdoor advertising, as well as direct mail, point-of-sale, public relations, and sponsorships. The Internet has its own unique characteristics. Contrary to what happens in other media, the message is rarely taken to the audience. It is seldom found positioned between popular features or interrupting a favorite show or placed along a well-traveled road. The audience must go to the marketer's website and virtually *seek out* the message. And the marketer must provide both directions and incentives to go there.

It is astonishing how many companies or individuals with websites take the *Field of Dreams* approach to their sites. In that popular film, a young man was told about a baseball field that would draw the legends of the game: "If you build it, they will come." So he builds the field and they come. It is a good enough movie. Alas, things don't quite work that way with Internet sites.

No one believes that if you produce a TV spot, everyone will see it, even if you run the spot several times on a popular prime-time program. It is assumed that some people will see it, but not all, and maybe not even all of the people who saw the hit program. One also does not assume that a great brochure will be seen or read until steps are taken to put it into the hands of people who might be interested in what it has to say.

Not so with the website.

In the marketing environment of the new century, many companies are so aggressively and zealously web-focused that they are ignoring opportunities to market to people with vehicles that were among their first-tier media choices in pre-Internet days.

For example, when it was suggested to one extremely media-savvy CEO that it was time to prepare a year-in-review press release (to revisit recent successes and try to get a mention in the many year-end wrap-up stories being written), the CEO's reply was, "Instead of putting the release out on the wire, let's just post it on our website."

After waiting a moment for his shock to subside, the marketer responded that posting information on the website was always a good idea, but since the media is being fed hundreds or thousands of pitches each day by companies trying to aggressively create a reputation for being "out there" and doing all they can to raise their profiles, posting your message *only* on the company website is a good strategy if one hopes to go unnoticed.

Members of the media (and even a company's strongest supporters and advocates) typically do not check the company website
for recently posted announcements on a frequent basis—certainly
not given the many overtures that are made to them in a normal day.
Even a phone call to suggest that the reporter or editor visit the site
will likely be viewed as an insulting suggestion from a lazy PR person. Marketers must take their story to their public. Waiting for or
expecting the public to come looking for news about what you have
to offer is not the real world—or even the cyberworld.

It is almost understandable that the CEO would have thought
his suggestion was less than ludicrous. Proponents of Internet marketing do in fact often treat their environment as if it exists in its
own universe. An example of this is the PR agency that sent holiday
greetings as E-mails, rather than sending the agency's traditional
Christmas card. Instead of snowflakes and Santa, a Simpletext greeting wished the recipient a happy holiday and requested a click on
the agency's website "to see what we've been doing."

Bah. Humbug.

That is almost as warm a holiday wish as "Check out our ad in
this Sunday's newspaper."

Without even a wistful thought about "peace on earth," this
greeting is a reflection of the strategy many marketers (both in-
house and agency) are recommending and employing. It is presented as a modern way to reach one's public, presumably because
it uses technology rather than postage stamps. To most businesses,
alas, anything that comes with the phrase "saves the cost of mailing" sounds like a good idea. Add the phrase "high-tech" and it has
sex appeal as well. But will it get people to look at your website?

Why should they?

Putting aside the fact that your E-mail has invaded their computer with a self-serving message disguised as a greeting card, what
is the incentive or motivation for anyone to take *their own* time to

go to *your* website to hear what you have to say, when they have others coming to them with the information up front and they don't have to work to get it? Plus, the other guy probably sent a very thoughtful card by Hallmark or American Greetings, with a no-strings-attached wish for peace and goodwill to all.

A company that has worked long and hard to create goodwill and a good reputation cannot afford to cut corners by using methods that make it look cheap, self-important, and disconnected from its public. This is especially the case for business-to-business companies, for whom relationships are more critical than for the manufacturer, retailer, or direct-to-consumer marketer, who typically doesn't maintain ties on such a personal level.

Know the Rules of the New Marketplace

Large numbers of E-mails sent unsolicited to lists of individuals or businesses are considered *spam*, electronic junk mail that is not only unwelcome, but in several states in the United States, illegal as well. E-mail marketing specialists have suggestions for getting around this, mainly variations on the idea of calling it something else,

Is a press release sent unsolicited to media organizations a violation of protocol? No, it is not. Many media organizations request an E-mail format rather than faxes, phone calls, or traditional mail.

What if, in addition to the media, the same press release is sent to shareholders in the company? That would be considered acceptable as well.

How about if the information went to those two groups and a list of security analysts that follow the industry? OK.

And if it went to a purchased list of prospective customers or "influentials"?

Here's where the light flashes and the machine starts beeping. The E-mail could be titled "A Holiday Greeting" or "A Report from the Chairman of the Board." Or it may be a friendly note asking you to click on and see all the exciting changes made in the company's website. But the fact is that a communication sent in bulk to a list of people, whether electronically or with a stamp, is usually regarded as junk mail.

Good marketers, when they want to impress people, do not just send a communication telling the person what steps to follow and where to go for information. *They send the information.*

A target market group should never be asked to work through steps to find out what you have to offer. Of course, the communication can include a line such as "Visit our website for news and features that can help _____." (Fill in the benefit your product, brand, or company can provide.)

Sending E-mails, just as with any other "mail" (Priority, Express, FedEx, UPS), can be effective and cost-efficient but should be used wisely.

Let's return to the issue of how to best market a press release. Posting a press release on the website, but not on the newswire, falls under the heading of "preaching to the choir." You want your information to be seen by your public, but you are disseminating it in a way that ensures it reaches mostly the people who already know you and support you—and may even already have the information.

There are reasons why companies put out press releases and why, in this Internet Age, individuals and companies still place ads in newspapers and magazines or on TV and radio and include 800 numbers or a street address. They do it to get noticed. The mere existence of a company's website is not a good enough reason for people to visit the site.

As with any other type of promotion, people need an offer or incentive to "check out the site." And then they need a reason to go back again.

Whether the company is launching a website or grappling with decisions about using other companies' sites, it should apply the same standard as it would use with other media:

- What/Who is my market?
- What media best reaches this market?
- What percentage of my media budget will this take relative to the percentage of the market it will reach?

There are similarities and distinctions in the media. Ad-sales reps for magazines (most of which, today, have both print and online editions) can offer persuasive arguments as to why their product cost-effectively reaches the audience you want to reach. So can ad reps from TV, radio, newspapers, direct marketing, and out-of-home promotions. Those arguments are still sketchy and unreliable when applied to online marketing.

Proponents of the Internet are also extremely comfortable showing their sense of elitism. They freely admit that this is not a market for everybody. People who do not use or revere personal computers are held in great disdain, regarded as a market not worth having.

The World Wide Web Is *Very* Wide— Know Where You're Going

In terms of reputation marketing, an Internet presence—or an intentional *lack* of presence—can define and position a brand, product, company, or other entity. Having a Web presence is viewed as a necessity for everyone from Victoria's Secret to the Louvre, the White House, Disney World, the pope, the National Rifle Association, and Chuck E. Cheese, to name just a few of the millions of site owners around the world.

Publications, associations, and foundations find that a website provides them with a display ad or directory listing for a fraction of what it would cost anywhere else. It's an opportunity to advance their reputations cost-efficiently.

Cities have websites for tourism and economic development. Businesses that once viewed themselves as merely small, local companies—too insignificant for television, given its high cost and huge audience outside of a small business's market zone—now maintain websites in the "borderless society" that constitutes a global marketplace.

Publicists see the Internet as a vast web of opportunity to target specific demographic segments efficiently, and for a fraction of the cost of advertising to the same segment in other media (which, ironically, would deliver only a fraction of the potential audience).

In terms of reputation marketing and positioning, there are in fact reasons why companies choose *not* to have a website.

Some companies are reluctant, unwilling, or unable to establish what they perceive as interactive relationships, since "doing it right" usually takes a trained staff and other resources that can be extremely costly. It's not just setting up the site, but what comes once it's set up—orders, E-mails, questions, and feedback—that many companies and institutions have no machinery in place to deal with. The volume of such communications can be significant. Although some people say a huge volume of mail and attention is the kind of problem they wish they had, they're very often wrong.

Other companies are swayed by the competitive aspect of having an Internet presence. Although website development and maintenance can be relatively modest in cost, they are not free. If one competitor allocates a large budget for creating and promoting a dazzling website, to what degree should others in the industry follow? The question is the same one companies face when considering ads and listings in professional directories, industry trade publications, and even the phone book. It comes down to what a company can afford relative to the perceived value and return on investment, and what it can afford *not* to do before its reputation begins to suffer.

Sometimes people make the case for a heavy Internet presence by suggesting that online, a small company can look as important and globally positioned as a much larger company, just by pumping up the color and sizzle of its website.

Although that is correct on a simple, basic level, it assumes that the visitor to the site will also visit every other site in the category and then undertake a thoughtful process of comparison.

Maybe, but maybe not.

Consider this: how many search engines contain your site's listing, and where do you rank among your competitors on various search engines' lists? If you have a truly exciting and colorful Web presentation, how long does it take to load before the visitor gets tired of waiting? To many visitors, even twenty or thirty seconds of waiting for the animation to kick in can seem like a very long time. Increasingly, websites are taking full advantage of the technology by linking to other sites that might appear to add value to the original site. They might, but even this useful, helpful device can be a double-edged sword. Will visitors who jump to a link come back? How many links are useful, and at what point does linking become counterproductive? In large office centers and shopping malls, everyone still wants the parking space closest to the door. Websites with too many links to other sites can be confusing and cumbersome, as well as adding to the "travel time."

But one of the most often-repeated concerns of the people and companies that hold back from Internet participation is the overall confusion of benefits vs. cost.

Several overarching questions need to be addressed:

- Is Internet advertising and/or website development merely another medium for marketing, similar to TV, radio, magazines, or the yellow pages?

- Or is the Internet an entirely new channel or method of doing business, such as mail order? Is it a single location or many locations?

- Is it a more effective approach to use E-mail rather than outbound telemarketing or traditional direct mail?

- In terms of its overall scope, does Internet marketing, because of its special requirements (namely, the need to develop a website, a technology system, and a response/fulfillment/tracking capability), constitute (1) a totally unique and specialized way of doing business and promoting a product, company, or message or (2) a distraction from the actual subject of the marketing effort because of the demands made on the visitor to the website—specifically, taking a self-service approach to gathering information and acting on it, as opposed to the marketer fully controlling the presentation process?

The answer, of course, is that there is no one answer. It all depends on the nature of the product or message; the marketer's relationship with the visitor, customer, or target audience; and how well the Internet, as a vehicle, serves the specific objectives of the marketing plan.

The Internet is decades old but is still in its infancy and will be for some time to come, as marketers continue to experiment with new uses and applications.

This much is known:

- Virtually every company, brand, institution, association, celebrity, and service provider operating in the current marketing environment perceives the need to have a website, if only because competitors in all categories appear to have websites. A website is a corporate brochure, and certainly there is an assumption that having a website presents opportunities to be taken advantage of.

- Having a website is not the same as having a presence on the World Wide Web. Developing a site is like creating that corporate brochure. It may very well look great, but until people see it and tell other people about it, it has no presence in the marketplace. This is where marketing comes in—making your target market aware of your site and the product or message the site is created to promote.

- Not everyone is connected to the Internet, owns a computer, or has access to a computer. And not everyone prefers to communicate or do business in this way. All marketing efforts that revolve around the Internet are largely irrelevant to the market segments that include these people.

- Despite a big push in the direction of banner ads for several years, research indicates that banner ads don't work. Almost everyone has attempted to use or to sell banners at some point, to enhance their Internet presence and generate revenue. It is every marketer's fantasy to take in enough income from the website to make it self-sustaining. This rarely happens. Alas, everyone wants to *sell* banners, but no one wants to *buy*. Most of the regularly seen banners are part of trades and cross-promotions that are largely regarded as intrusive and a nuisance.

- The Internet is a new marketplace that contains many old features, repackaged and renamed. For example, in viral marketing (which is considered a dynamic and innovative concept), E-mails—instead of paper mailings with high postage fees—are sent in large numbers to an affinity audi-

ence. In another context this would have been described as
"mailing to a qualified list."

- Internet usage is heavily tilted toward younger market segments. This is good news if those generations are the desired
  market. But if the target is not "plugged in," Internet marketing in almost any form can be costly and useless. This
  again underscores the importance of knowing the composition of your market. Luckily, in a business-to-business situation, chances improve. You are then marketing to the
  people who will take the message to others.

For marketers who are eager to build or change a corporate
image or reputation, the Internet is a viable component in a strategy, but rarely should the *entire* strategy be Internet-based.

Consider the fact that most people are aware of specific websites (out of several million sites in existence) because they have seen
them referred to in print ads, on TV, or on billboards. Most packaging now includes the address of the company's website, for people who apparently can't get enough information about their
toothpaste, pen, or sunglasses. Few people exposed to the existence
of these sites ever actually visit them, but through the reference: (1)
the company appears to be participating in what the modern world
has created; (2) the Web itself is being endorsed as credible, because
so many major entities believe they must be represented on it; and
(3) people will feel that it just actually might be helpful one day to
know about it.

What We Know About the Net

The collapse of the highly oversaturated, overhyped dot-coms was
actually a very positive occurrence (although the companies that

tanked would not agree) because it thinned the herd, leaving stronger, more efficiently operated companies to take their place among the various venture capitalists' flavors of the month.

Many people are familiar with the names of products and companies that they have never used or will ever use. The fact that they know the names of these companies is the result of a corporate-image marketing campaign, which may have used advertising, public relations, direct mail, event sponsorship, or (now) the Internet.

Using your website to collect information about the likes, dislikes, and opinions of people who visit your site is not only useful in focusing your product or service, but in providing press-release material or ad copy that can, again, shape and support the reputation you seek to establish. Such information, although hardly objective or authoritative, can help define your image.

Linking your website to sites of companies that have the image you want can provide you with not only the connections themselves (which will presumably offer something of value), but with an opportunity to promote the *association* of the links with your product or company, stressing how important these connections are to your constituency.

Offhandedly publicizing the association of unrelated (and unassociated) companies is not without precedent. For years, companies would run a one-time ad in a regional edition of *The Wall Street Journal* or *Time* magazine, and forever after promotions would carry a snipe reminding readers that the ad is the same one "As seen in *Time* magazine." This was meant to impart a certain degree of importance and prominence to the product through its association with an important and prominent media entity.

On any given day, only a few people may actually read a particular story in *Salon.com*, *Inside.com*, or the *Drudge Report*, but millions become aware that such a story exists once it—and its source—are referenced on a network TV newscast or talk show or quoted in the press. Not only the *appearance* of an ad or an item on the Internet, but *where* on the Internet it appeared, is important to your reputation. Just as there is an implied sense of importance when a subject appears in *Time*, whether in a story or an ad, there will be an implied sense of importance if your name appears on a prestigious website.

In the future, links on companies' websites to the sites of other companies or organizations will not only be convenient for the user, they will help create reputations for some organizations by the company they keep.

In some instances, simply making certain that your name is in the databases of major search engines will be enough. That's no small task, however. Powerful engines such as Yahoo! or AltaVista reach millions of Internet users, but there are hundreds of search engines on the Internet (a fact that many people overlook). Your reputation will not be enhanced measurably if you are only known to the fifty or so *least*-used engines.

Advertisers know that to have an impact, an ad must be seen. A merchandising campaign should always include—on mailers, flyers, signs, and packaging—the "As seen in (or *on*) _____" snipe. Radio spots should direct the audience to "Look for our ad in _____." Similarly, an Internet presentation only becomes a presence when people are made aware, through thoughtful marketing, of your being there.

"Word of mouth" knowledge of an Internet presence can usually be traced back to a reference in a newspaper or magazine, or a reference on radio or TV. One day, online marketing may be fully confined to its own medium, but as long as the public still watches TV or reads newspapers, listens to radio, looks at billboards, and opens its mail, the Internet and the World Wide Web should be regarded as parts of the larger media universe.

SUMMARY OF CHAPTER FIVE

- The degree to which your target market is online should guide the extent to which you choose to participate.

- Companies that have done well in catalog or mail-order businesses tend to do better online than companies that drew traffic primarily because of their locations in particular buildings, malls, or other prime locations.

- Do not expect your target market to come to your website just because it's there any more than customers will call you just because you have a phone. Your site must be marketed as if it were a product or a business location that requires traffic-building. But these efforts to become visible should not overshadow the product or message that you originally developed the site to provide.

- Decide whether your website is to *promote* your business or *be* your business. Remember that for most products, services, or information, not 100 percent of the market is online, and some segments likely never will be.

- Linking your website to the websites of companies or other entities that have the reputation you want is a way to accelerate the association of their reputations with yours. Create something of value and link to other similarly valuable sites.

CHAPTER SIX

Damage Control

Changing a "Bad Reputation"

> Rumor can fly halfway around the world
> before truth can get its pants on.
> —*attributed to Cordell Hull*

Saying that a company has a "bad reputation" might seem to be a rather general statement. In some respects, it is. Just as beauty can be said to be "in the eye of the beholder," reputations can be viewed differently by different entities. For example, a company that is labeled "slow-paying" by many of its suppliers may pay some of its other suppliers very promptly, perhaps even in advance. Maybe the company has a formula for how it schedules its payments: small or independent companies, or those that offer discounts for prompt payment, get paid first. Or perhaps it's the opposite—big companies with greater leverage get paid first.

A bad reputation may also result when word gets around that the company has a history of accepting merchandise or services and then—after the fact—renegotiating costs. Or perhaps it becomes known as a "revolving-door operation," if executives or employees leave the company far sooner than is normal for that particular industry or business. The company may have experienced union problems or been accused of fostering a hostile work environment.

A company or business acquires a bad reputation when it becomes known for something negative—anything from being hit with a lawsuit charging racial or sexual discrimination to charges of polluting, manufacturing faulty products, price-fixing, bribing public officials, to simply failing to honor its guarantees. Having a bad reputation does not necessarily mean that the company is *guilty* of any wrongdoing; it means a widespread *perception* exists that the company is guilty. Sometimes the company in question is doing everything right, but it's being victimized and discredited by competitors, special-interest groups, or disgruntled current or former employees.

A Casual Regard for the Truth

For decades, the occasional report of a fingernail (or worse) found in a hot dog would be met with a raised eyebrow as the listener reached for more mustard. People cut the average business a lot of slack. Although some people would pout and protest over some slight or slur, corporations for the most part could take a hit and keep on moving.

That was true until the 1990s, when—in technical terms—the wheel fell off. Then a rumor, even a hint of a scandal, could destroy more than a few reputations. It was a time of "open season" on the reputations of the mightiest and most powerful individuals and corporations in American society. Perfectly solid companies, associations, institutions, and prominent people who never needed to be concerned for their public images were sent reeling. Suddenly (or so it seemed) the American Medical Association, the American Bar Association, the U.S. military establishment, and churches of a dozen separate denominations were being profiled unfavorably on the evening news and in multipart newspaper stories across the United States. Respected institutions were shaken and their individual and collective public disapproval ratings were soaring.

"How could this happen?" they wondered. Each institution had believed it was as beloved as, well, the sun and Florida orange juice.

And who ever knew there was such a thing as a "public disapproval rating" anyway?

Who is in charge of it? How often does it come out? Can one get a copy of it, or does it only go to Chris Matthews at MSNBC?

One day, reports emerge that say everyone hates Microsoft because it is too huge and powerful and the government should teach all those young billionaire punks in the suburbs of Seattle a lesson. A day later, "new reports" say Microsoft isn't actually that bad and *did* in fact revolutionize much of how technology and communication come together, and critics who resent the company's tremendous success should just grow up and get over themselves.

Which side actually presents a true picture? On which day? And who produced and paid for these "reports"?

What effect, if any, did either report have on the company's stock, and if it had no effect, why not? *Priceline* or *Moneyline*—whose news do you take to the bank? And does it matter, when a company's stock is down 90 percent from its high of a year earlier.

An abundance of news sources feel free to report critical information without attribution, in their haste to be first with the big breaking story of the day. If the story turns out to be different than the report, or nothing at all, another "report" of a "correction" can always be issued, along with a reminder that the public should always exercise caution when acting on news reports without first checking all the facts.

Uh-huh.

When a news organization reports that "unconfirmed information" is being circulated (because, in the event it might be accurate, no one wants to be the last one out with the story), the rest of the marketplace has an interesting array of choices:

- Does anyone dare ignore a big juicy rumor—even though it was sent out to an audience of potentially millions of people, many of them very influential—*specifically* as an unconfirmed report?
- Does the subject of the report—a person, company, brand, or organization—dare to refuse to comment on such a widely publicized unconfirmed report? And if the comment is that there is no truth whatsoever to the rumor, does anyone believe the comment in an era when truth is routinely denied in courtrooms and Senate chambers on live television with the whole world watching?
- Doesn't the denial of a rumor consitute the creation of a news story in itself?

In focusing on reputation marketing and management, it is important to be aware of the following things: (1) that a large and still-growing number of special-interest groups exist to promote their own agenda; (2) that individuals, companies, and groups in the United States file more lawsuits than are filed in any other country in the world; (3) that many of these lawsuits are filed for the express purpose of making a point, usually at the expense of some individual or company (and its reputation); and (4) that very often the plaintiff's first action after filing a lawsuit is to go on the offensive by issuing a press release, calling a press conference, or beginning a so-called media blitz. The plaintiff is trying to define the issue, control the discussion, and create an outpouring of support for him- or herself.

Initiators of these actions have (at least) four simultaneous objectives:

1. Make their point
2. Publicize the fact that they are out there making their point
3. Create or enhance their reputation by emphasizing that they have taken an action
4. Underscore their leadership by publicizing the action

The Media Has a Very Large Appetite for Bad News

In this regard, there are some points worth noting regarding the media:

- News coverage has been called unfair and uneven almost since its beginnings. Reputations have been ruined along the way—and all that was before the world had cable and the Internet.
- Without question, standards in news reporting have changed dramatically. The concept of unbiased, objective reporting has been de-emphasized in favor of more colorful presentations that encourage a point of view.
- Lines have blurred between "hard news" and "soft news": features, profiles, and documentaries.
- Individuals and businesses alike have become so aware of the effect a news segment, profile, or even a mere mention

in the right media environment can have that they have become both more media-savvy and more willing to comply with media requests, sometimes even acting against their own best interests.

I wrote the following in an earlier book called *Image Marketing*:

> For years an old adage held, "I don't care what you write about me, just spell my name right." One can only wonder what sort of mentality truly believes that "any publicity is good publicity." Certainly not anyone who counts on the goodwill of others to support a career or a business. The concept of "spin control"—putting the best face on a story—certainly does not presuppose that *any* publicity is good publicity. Indeed, some entrepreneurs, investors, and others pay press agents to help keep them *out* of the public eye.

The high cost of doing business and the intensity of competition in virtually every industry have contributed to an environment in which instant results are increasingly the order of the day. This has made the role of the media even more important than it was already perceived to be.

Although marketers promoting a company, a product, or a cause might have adopted a strategy of working an industry or a region incrementally to win support, the emphasis is now on getting "out there" with any and all possible exposure as quickly as possible. This means, ideally, the full media showcase of TV, print, radio, and now Internet exposure. Such exposure increases awareness, and greater awareness leads to perceptions and images being formed; these, in turn, help establish a reputation.

A CEO's interview by Office.com, a CBS online venture, is in some quarters accorded the same value as an interview on the CBS television network, especially because the piece can be accessed on personal computers around the world for an open-ended period of time.

But the more eager a marketer is to score the big media hit, the greater the exposure is for *negative* press for several reasons:

- Attention begets attention. This is a double-edged sword, as the saying goes. On the good side, being profiled in major media increases the chances of your becoming better known to other major media. But very often, such attention prompts a reporter or producer who was not first with the story, but doesn't want to ignore it, to explore ways of presenting "the story behind the story" or a different take on the subject. This may not include information that is in the subject's best interests. It is not at all uncommon for a media organization that did not discover a story or subject (or have it submitted for consideration first) to "go negative," looking for unfavorable or unflattering information to report. The organization thereby suggests there is greater value in *its* version of the story, even if that version wasn't the first exposure to the subject.

- The overwhelming amount of media coverage is superficial. While this may seem like an unfair generalization, it is nonetheless true. Consider a typical news story or segment that runs between 150 and 1,000 words. A phone interview with a reporter may last from fifteen minutes to an hour or more. The interviewee will see the essence of that session reported as anything from a fragment of a quote to several sentences—presented, by necessity, out of context. Reporters and editors are supposed to be able to summarize or extract

the important points of an interview. But quite often, the
most important or strongest point is in the eye of the
beholder, meaning the reporter or editor's selected quote
might not be the same one selected by a company PR person. Reasons for the variation can be anything from sloppy
editing to bad reporting to the failure of the interviewee to
get his or her point across succinctly.

- Perhaps the speaker assumed that the reporter had been
  better briefed, done more homework, or knew more about
  the subject than he or she actually did. Big mistake. There
  used to be an old school rule—*never assume*. Today, this
  rule appears to have been abandoned. It is always risky to
  assume that an interviewer knows and understands what you
  mean and perhaps even agrees with you—especially when
  your information will have to be presented briefly, concisely,
  and without elaboration.

- Bad news is usually more popular and interesting than good
  news. This fact has actually been well-known and largely
  accepted for a long time, yet as in the previous point, it is
  still often assumed that a reporter or interviewer is favorably
  disposed to a subject and wants to make that subject look
  good. *Very* big mistake.

    This does not mean that a reporter, a request for infor-
mation, or an interview should be handled with suspicion or
hostility. It does mean, however, that such inquiries should
be dealt with in a professional manner that emphasizes a
strong, positive position. Allow for the possibility that the
genial reporter is not a friend whose main responsibility is
to look out for you. The top five stories on a typical TV newscast or in each edition of the daily paper are normally hard
news (read: bad news) stories, which reflect something dark,

negative, or accusatory about their subjects. Research indicates that audiences find bad news more engaging than a recitation of good deeds and virtuous conduct by celebrities, public officials, or the friendly staff of your local post office.

- If bad news is not what the marketer wants to see conveyed, the best time to plan on how to deal with it is not *after* the story has appeared.

Some individuals or companies want to be seen as mavericks, muckrakers, antagonists, whistle-blowers, or just controversial and generally going against the grain. Although this may be more interesting than a six-minute review of "quiet competence," there are risks to staking out such positions. The subject may win some support from disaffected members of the public who like to root for the underdog, but may also alienate many others. Such positioning can also appear contrived, affected, insincere, and self-serving. It may result in receiving short-term attention, but over the long term, it will earn a reputation for being opportunistic and unsavory—qualities rarely of benefit when promoting a product, company, brand, cause, individual, or issue.

Opportunities for "Interest Groups" Are Many and Lucrative

The term *special-interest group* used to mean professionals such as lobbyists, trade associations, and unions. Now, a special-interest group can be almost anyone with an issue, a fund-raising letter, and a mailing list.

In *Crisis Marketing: When Bad Things Happen to Good Companies*, I noted that: "Just as fads and trends and 'new and improved' products are a fact of marketing life, so are the crises. . . . The fur industry, tobacco companies, drug laboratories—evil incarnate or victims of exploitive pressure groups?"

In reality, in business today it is not paranoia to believe there is someone "out to get you." Is it coincidence or is there a relationship between the facts that (1) we are in the most litigious time in history; (2) we are in a totally media-pervasive environment; and (3) there is a special-interest group for every concern, vocation, avocation, person, place, or thing. Gun owners, overweight people, short people, vegetarians, airline passengers, cat lovers, librarians, and virtually any other subject one can name have groups to represent them, not in the sense of a club or trade group or professional association, but as a special-interest group in the way the term has come to be defined. These groups exist primarily to create pressure through numbers, whether they are running ads, directing demonstrations, initiating letter-writing campaigns and petition drives, calling press conferences and issuing press releases (to announce the launching or results of letter-writing campaigns and petition drives), and discussing "demands."

The aim of critics, pressure groups, and others who do not wish you well is to advance their reputations for being do-gooders acting on the side of right, while simultaneously calling a particular company or target subject's reputation into question.

This reality has come about and gained momentum in part because there are an expanding set of media that are willing and eager (and often in desperate need) to cover subjects of interest, especially controversies. There is also a long list of lawyers who are hungry for exposure and attention, which they can get from contacting this myriad of media entities to announce that lawsuits are being contemplated or filed on behalf of some special-interest group or cause. Additionally, the lawyers are hoping to come out of the episode with a strong reputation that can be exploited at a later time.

But perhaps the most significant reason that such special-interest efforts and campaigns have become so routine is that they are frequently effective—enough so as to encourage others to employ the same tactics.

Tactics Change as Old Good Guys Are Called Bad Guys

Who could have thought it possible to win a multibillion-dollar judgment against an industry by admitting to ignoring warning labels on products, and then suing for experiencing the exact damage that the warning said would result if it was ignored?

People who didn't like a particular television program used to simply not watch it, whereas it is now extremely common to issue press releases and threaten boycotts of the program's sponsors, as well as of the TV station or network that carried the program. Although the reason for the boycott is usually an offensive program, increasingly even a normal evening-news program will be accused of carrying excessive accounts of actual events that are deemed objectionable and, by the way, are being reported by someone who also is offensive.

There are clear examples of individuals and companies that have suffered damage to their reputations as a result of unfounded rumors and unwarranted attacks. What is unfortunate is that by merely claiming an intent to provide information, an accuser or reporter need only insert the words "allegedly" or "reportedly" or "is rumored to have" before a comment and can then follow it with almost anything.

The More Outrageous the Charge, the Greater the Coverage

Claims of offenses do not have to make sense. Consider:

At various times, both McDonald's and Procter & Gamble have been accused of being somehow aligned with the "Church of Satan." Although the charges were absurd, it was necessary for the companies to respond in the interests of protecting their respective reputations. In so doing, they not only spent a lot of money, but gave more attention to the stories. It is fair to assume that some people, having heard an allegation, will always hold doubts about the veracity of its denial.

In the broadest sense, were McDonald's or Procter & Gamble's reputations hurt by the "Church of Satan" allegations?

No—for two main reasons. First, the sheer silliness of the assertion made it hard for almost everyone to accept. Second, both companies had spent years focusing on building consumer trust and credibility. The public, having witnessed a history of good works and deeds, was predisposed in favor of the companies. Anyone wanting to smear their reputations would have to make a very strong case indeed, which of course in these instances, the accusers were hard-pressed to do.

When it was reported that hypodermic syringes were found in cans of Pepsi, suggesting unimaginable levels of risk to consumers, the company responded swiftly and confidently with unequivocal denials and bottling-plant videos showing how such an occurrence could not have been even remotely possible.

Was Pepsi hurt? No, because (1) again, the allegation itself was so absurd; (2) the response by Pepsi was quick and sure, flatly denouncing the claims as untrue; and (3) while not as well known for its charitable endeavors as McDonald's, Pepsi was widely regarded as being respectful of its largely young customer base (the

"Pepsi Generation") and careful in managing its image, identifying its brand with celebrities its core constituency admired and respected. Such a company, it logically followed, would never permit so serious a lapse in quality control, one that would compromise its reputation and tarnish its image with its valued customers.

The case of the national restaurant chain that was charged with practicing racial discrimination is another matter. After initially denying that such practices were company policy, the chain's management finally offered to settle the question by making amends.

First, unlike any of the companies that take great care in creating goodwill *before* having to deal with crisis issues, this company had no accumulated goodwill it could draw upon. Second, the offer to make amends sounded suspicious in the way it was represented, as if it were coming not from people who care about their customers and value their goodwill, but from a settlement drafted by the company's lawyers. It may as well have begun with the phrase "Without admitting or denying the charges, we do hereby agree . . ."

Let's say, for the sake of argument, that your company really *did* screw up—*big time*. A good response would be not to *say* you're sorry (in a transparent, carefully worded legal brief), but to *show* it. Create an event to sponsor—something that will tell customers at the community level that the company is not of, for, and about "bad guys." Sponsoring music, art, athletics, and other events, with prizes of scholarships or recognition, indicates that a company wants to enthusiastically identify itself with its customers and communities in an involved, supportive, and positive way. Underwriting programs for day-care centers or senior-citizen centers, or creating promotions that offer merchandise (CDs, posters, caps, et cetera) with proceeds going to support local or national youth organizations or scholarship funds, will make a very positive statement.

The public may long remember that your company was charged with inappropriate behavior, but over time, by building a solid record of showing customers how much the company values what the public thinks, it is possible to change people's minds enough that your reputation becomes one in which either (1) the company got a bad rap or (2) having done wrong, the company went the extra mile to make up for its mistakes with actions, not merely press releases.

Doing Too Little Too Late

Too often, individuals and companies don't come to appreciate the value of a good reputation until they are in trouble and looking for someone to come forward and offer a kind word on their behalf. Trying to convince the public that a company is a valuable asset to its community is a hard case to make if the company's entire history suggests it hasn't cared what people thought.

Building a good reputation before you're in trouble is a better business strategy than trying to change a bad reputation after you're in trouble.

It is simply good business sense to create a reputation that invites respect, support, and loyalty—attributes that are invaluable in times of trouble. This seems simple and obvious, yet many companies continue to devote few or no resources to community relations, shareholder relations, governmental relations, and even the most basic levels of public relations, choosing to respond to serious questions and concerns with a cold "no comment." Sometimes, it becomes clear that such positioning can come back to bite.

The powerful Microsoft, the company that arguably shifted the entire focus of business in the 1990s, totally ignored the fact that its reputation—both inside and outside the technology industry—was one of extreme arrogance. It shrugged at allegations of heavy-handed business dealings and anticompetitive practices and largely dismissed complaints about its lack of customer service. Only when a government antitrust suit threatened to severely curtail Microsoft's operations did the world get TV commercials featuring the company's CEO in a sweater, looking much like a boyish, friendly grad student, implying that his hugely prosperous company was an example of the American Dream, proof of the righteousness of the capitalist system, and reminding viewers how important it was that everyone should care about what happened to it.

Although the media was glad to take the company's money and run the spots, the general feeling was that no one, including Microsoft employees, believed a word of it. More than a year after the ad campaign began, the company was still regarded as arrogant and indifferent to complaints or criticism. The ads were a transparent attempt to soften a harsh opinion of the company prior to a federal judge's ruling on the fate of Microsoft and the circumstances under which it would be allowed to operate. The judge, like the TV audience, was unmoved by this insincere display of "too little, too late."

How might the company have responded differently to its problem? First, a *recognition by management* of the situation would have been helpful. A print-ad campaign could have acknowledged that the company had grown so large so fast that its customer-service practices were now out of date and were being overhauled. E-mails about specific grievances could have been invited. The company could have published the top ten most frequently noted complaints and announced a timetable for corrective action, which would very likely have had some influence on the judge's own response.

Instead of the clichéd CEO-in-sweater-reading-a-cue-card TV spot, the very same CEO could have been sitting at a round table, answering questions from users of his products—students, secretaries, small-business operators, and so on. Even heavily scripted and edited, the campaign would have been more substantive than the noninformative patter in the fluffy spots that impressed no one. Or an ad could have presented the company's CEO in a dialogue with other industry leaders who did not have issues with how he conducted his business, thereby implying that the critics may have constituted a jealous minority.

Microsoft is a preeminent American company. As such, it should be a model for other companies in its industry. Incidentally, that would serve its own interests quite well—particularly with its employees and stockholders.

Another important point has to do with the technology industry itself. So many young companies, run by so many young people, have not had the proper benefit of experience that comes with time and testing. A new software producer, a dot-com, or an Internet company that attracts large sums of venture capital and enjoys a successful IPO is likely to have a highly distorted sense of its corporate self, given a universe where the basis for a reputation is often only a matter of the day's closing stock price or merger announcement.

Microsoft, Apple, AOL, Amazon.com, e-Toys, eBay, Yahoo!, AltaVista, and other companies that enjoy "flavor-of-the-month" status are often overvalued and undervalued in the same season by analysts who may have a short-term performance record to judge, but cannot factor in the company's reputation—because the company itself never actually gave much thought to the matter or took interest in establishing a reputation. At no time is this as obvious and troublesome as when the tide turns against a company, brand, or product and there is nothing to which the company can anchor its name for defense. *It has no reputation* to speak of, since its success was derived from having a product that was given a chance and succeeded for a time, thanks to good timing and a strong market, but without any real focused effort by the company.

Think First, Act Early

The factors that can be used to save a company's reputation in times of crisis can be used to even greater advantage in the event that the crisis does *not* occur. Before the reputation-saving process is needed, it should be in place and the company should be observing some very elementary principles that are, in fact, simply part of a good marketing strategy:

- **Do something good.** That's not just a glib statement. People and companies that are associated with good deeds or worthy causes become known for such associations and earn a reputation that reflects these actions. Whether the issue is literacy, the environment, the sponsorship of homeless shelters, food pantries for the needy, toys for tots, or recording books for the blind, doing good works benefits many people—especially the doer.

    Note: It is important that motives be sound, even if slightly transparent. That is, no one begrudges a person credit for doing good deeds, but not if the act is so contrived and insincere as to insult the intelligence of the public.

- **Stand for something.** A reputation comes from the public knowing something about you—that you have quality products, fair prices, integrity, a good guarantee, product service, community service, or commitment to a cause.

- **Take credit.** Put a plaque on the school gym, your name on Little League shirts, your page in the opera or theater program, and publicize your donations to the shelter. No one likes braggarts who take more credit than is deserved, but generosity or good work, service, or contributions should not be anonymous.

- **Understand the goals and services combination.** A
  wise marketer once noted that smart marketing will help you
  get the customer, but good service is what will help you *keep*
  the customer. And a reputation for good service is something
  others say about you, not something you say about yourself.

But what if you fail to dodge the bullet and indeed become
caught up in a crisis situation? Let's say your company is sued for
wrongdoing by a disgruntled employee. Perhaps you are even
charged with questionable practices by a fully *gruntled* employee.
Whatever the situation, you are the lead story on the evening
news—or you expect to be.

- Publicly acknowledge the problem as quickly as possible—
  ideally, before it becomes news to which you must respond.
- Define the story. By presenting your version first, you have
  a better chance of controlling the tone and possibly the
  direction of the story.
- Announce that you are investigating any reports or allegations—and then make sure that you do.
- Designate a single spokesperson who will be available to
  present your side of the story and answer questions. Having
  more than one spokesperson can result in conflicting comments that undercut your position.
- Present and maintain the positioning of your company or
  issue in a larger context than the current problem.
- Keep your own people, *at every level*, well informed. It is
  troubling and embarrassing for them to be asked about the
  problem by friends, family, and acquaintances and know
  nothing more than what they've read in the newspaper.
  These people can be your main source of support, and as
  your internal base, you owe them an early and honest expla-

nation of the facts. Your reputation as a good employer and your ability to recruit good people in the future could hinge on this.

Act like a Leader

In times of crisis, your customers, clients, stockholders, members of your industry or profession, the public, and the media will be taking note of how you respond. Act as if you think the whole world is watching, because it very well might be. At such times, act like a leader.

Although advertising is the most efficient way of reaching the largest audience in the time, place, and manner of your choice, with a controlled message—and without questions, challenges, or rebuttal—there are times when an ad program should be suspended or reconsidered. For instance, if you represent an airline and one of your planes has crashed—even if it was not a "worst-case situation"—it is appropriate to suspend advertising as you deal with the crisis. Although some people may argue that the appearance of "business as usual" sends a good message, that is not always the case and it can easily be misinterpreted. Typically upbeat ads showing passengers enjoying air travel are wholly inappropriate when a tragedy, near-tragedy, or potential litigation is on everyone's mind. Don't leave room for your public to perceive you as insensitive. Even if you represent an airline and one of your *competitor's* planes has crashed, consider briefly suspending your own ads while public attention is focused on the airline disaster, discussing what sorts of things could have gone wrong. Put out a statement supporting overall airline safety and express concern for the victims. You will be regarded as "taking the high road" and acting in a statesman-like way.

If you are representing a chain of restaurants, hotels, car dealerships, or any multiple-location operations or franchises, consider the circumstances under which you might do better to suspend advertising. Someone may have been attacked or injured at one of your locations. Obviously, this should not be an indictment of every location or the company itself, but an ad appearing in the same edition of a newspaper or on the same TV or radio newscast that reports the bad-news story can be embarrassing and can draw more attention to the story.

Shift the focus away from the company property. A marketer's responsibility is to protect the reputation of the company to the highest degree possible. Obviously, if security is lax at the location and/or throughout the chain, that is likely to come out. It is a smarter course to acknowledge the problem, get on with a solution, and fairly (and swiftly) settle specific claims to the extent that is possible. But there is nothing inappropriate about steering media focus away from the company when the problem is part of a larger societal issue. Competitors will likely be doing everything possible to keep the focus on the company in trouble and not allow the public to think that such situations might just as well have occurred at one of the competitors' properties.

Note that this strategy assumes that the issue is, in fact, about random acts of violence or other situations that actually could have happened anywhere—a parking garage or lot, stairways of public buildings, in parks, transit shelters, and so on. If an incident occurs in an area known for having a high crime rate, or in a place where such incidents have occurred less than infrequently, the situation is not a marketing problem and needs solutions other than what this book offers. Security and safety of customers are issues that can be exploited for better or worse. Take steps to assure it is for better and correct any deficiencies to the degree that is possible.

If a company has worked to create a positive corporate image and a good reputation, isolated incidents will probably not have a lasting effect. Indeed, a long period of time passing without occurrences of trouble reinforces the company's contention that the issue was an isolated and random act. The day after a major airline disaster, thousands of people are getting on planes, believing (and betting their lives) that the likelihood of another such incident is extremely remote.

Reputations that can be used to great advantage in cases of damage control are built on trust and factors that inspire trust, such as:

- the *history* of the company, its management, its product, or its service
- the *image* of the company as it evolved during that history, as well as the record of how any past problems were resolved
- the *public's opinion*, pro and con, of the founder, manager, or spokesperson
- the *competition*—under normal circumstances, how you are perceived in comparison to others who do what you do in terms of price, quality, value, and image, as well as how you conduct business in times of crisis
- *word-of-mouth* reports as compared to advertising, PR, or media coverage you generate—what people are *actually* saying about you versus what you are saying about yourself
- your policy on *guarantees, warranties*, or *customer satisfaction* in general—basically the public's perception of how much you care about what they think of you and how far you are willing to go to please customers
- *convenience*, an often-neglected, but extremely important, consideration in building a reputation for service and

integrity. Make it as easy as possible for people to do business with you (get information, get delivery, handle returns). Many businesses with fine products at good prices will ignore customer complaints that "they make it so hard to do business with them." Special orders, reservations, layaway plans, loyalty points (frequent flyer/frequent diner programs), gift-certificate purchases and redemptions, membership discounts and benefits, coupons, priority seating, twenty-four-hour phone service, gift-wrapping, credit-card and check policy, business hours, service hot lines, competitive pricing, VIP services, personal attention, special plans for students, employees, government workers, and seniors . . . all these concepts have been tried with mixed success. They are all good ideas in theory: the degree of their success is dependent on the degree to which such plans are taken seriously and managed efficiently. A "personal banker" whose "personal customers" include most of the people doing business with the bank isn't quite what customers had been led to expect. "Priority service" that means "Your call will be taken in the order in which it was received" is not much of a priority. Staying open most days only until 5 P.M., when your customers are working at their own jobs and couldn't possibly reach you in time, is not offering much in the way of convenience, even if price and quality are competitive.

Do What It Takes to Win Goodwill . . . and Business

Too many businesses, from hospitals to insurance companies to banks, dry cleaners, and fast-food restaurants, respond to customer questions, concerns, or complaints with phrases such as *"Our* policy on that is _____" instead of "How can I help you?"

Every company and business needs organization and structure, but increasingly this is being focused around the needs and convenience of the company and not the public that keeps the business in business. Such positioning is sure to provide a shortcut to a bad reputation.

The late department-store tycoon Marshall Field is credited with the phrase and the policy "The customer is always right." This is in contrast to more contemporary store policies, which seem to take not only an opposite view ("The customer is always wrong"), but one that says "The customer is probably trying to get something for nothing."

Such a policy does not exactly evoke memories of *Miracle on 34th Street*, the classic story of the Macy's department store Santa Claus who put the children's happiness first by sending customers to whichever store had the best deal, thereby generating more business and a wonderful reputation for Macy's.

Say what you will about customers becoming more rude than ever and demanding more for less, but consider these facts:

- It is the companies' and service providers' claims, ads, and assorted inflated representations that have caused so much of the public to believe they would indeed *get* more for less.
- Marshall Field, in taking the approach that held "The customer is always right," built an enormously successful chain of retail department stores, attracting customers who were both *willing to pay more* for the promise of better service and demonstrated through the years an appreciably *greater degree of loyalty*, insisting that they would "only shop at Field's."

For generations, Marshall Field's maintained a *reputation* for superior service, higher prices, and an upscale clientele—whether or not those things were true.

For some people, one bad meal at a restaurant or inflated fees for parking is enough to put a business on bad paper. Generally, it does (or should take) something considerably more serious, such as:

- A scandal or an association with scandal. Sometimes a fine product has to struggle in the dark shadow of an unsavory executive, as in the case of the Helmsley Organization, which was well-regarded for operating some of the world's finest hotels and real-estate properties. Meanwhile, Mrs. Helmsley (who lived a life of self-indulgence and enjoyed seeing herself in the company's ads) went to prison for tax evasion and was deemed the "Queen of Mean" for her reported cruelty to members of her personal staff.

- A prolonged strike, or open displays of hostility between labor and management, can create the image of a company that is poorly run, regardless of the company's profit performance or record of efficiency. Such an image is bad for employee morale—which affects performance as much as anything can—and hurts recruiting efforts, as well as leaving bad impressions for securities analysts and potential investors to digest.

- Behavior that prompts accusations (or worse, *proof*) of being a polluter of the environment, engaging in acts of cruelty to animals (as in some testing labs), or exploiting underage or underpaid foreign laborers are quick ways to alienate the public, as are age, sexual, or racial discrimination; sexual harassment; lapses in quality control or safety procedures that result in injury or death; knowingly producing or distributing a dangerous or questionable product and intentionally withholding warnings of potential risks; and being party to any action that knowingly violates legal or ethical standards or puts a person or persons at risk.

Attempt to Avoid Controversy

There are actually companies that welcome media exposure of any kind, viewing it as a means of increasing the public's awareness, even if it *is* as the subject of controversy. Nonsense. The very fact that crisis management has become such a significant area of specialization in the public-relations field is testament to the frequency with which such situations arise in the course of doing business. No matter who you are or what you do, on a large or small scale, there is someone out there who would like to advance his or her agenda at your expense. The number of people taking legal action for the most odd, trivial, or "nuisance" situations is high enough that businesses and prominent individuals should be concerned.

- The lawsuit filed against a local park board by the father (a lawyer) of a boy who did not get to be on the Little League team of his choice is absurdly trivial, yet both the legal profession and the community in question received weeks of publicity that left people shaking their heads about the level of sanity and worthiness of both. This is not good publicity for lawyers, who are already more than a little defensive when it comes to their reputations.
- A cable company or other service provider fails to respond with service in a reasonable amount of time, and hate mail is on the Internet, leading to an item in the newspaper or on local TV. Quirky? "Human interest"? Not to the businesses or professionals involved. To many companies, being the butt

of a "funny little story in the news today" is not funny at all, especially when these items gain wider circulation as human-interest stories on network programs.

On a crisis level, how can a cable guy's being late be compared to a product-tampering case that leads to the deaths of innocent people? They should obviously *not* be compared. There are big stories and little stories. But regardless of whether the issue is a headline-making crisis or a word-of-mouth nuisance, if it keeps customers and supporters away even for a little while, business should be tuned in and tuned up.

It is important to build and maintain a good reputation by doing good works, giving good service, publicizing what you do, and modestly taking and accepting credit for it. This is a matter of creating a *reservoir of goodwill* from which you might draw at a later time.

Coming Back from Damage to Your Reputation

After the bad news has been passed around—whether via the Internet, front pages, or back fence—is it too late to salvage a reputation, company, brand, or cause?

The answer is usually *no*.

The public has demonstrated an amazing capacity to forgive and, if not to forget, to at least allow another chance.

Consider the enormous number of product recalls over the past half-century—cars, toys, cartons of milk, and cans of tuna, for example. A benevolent public has shown a willingness in countless cases to accept an apology, a refund, or a promise and go on to purchase again from the same manufacturer, distributor, or service provider.

Indeed, many crisis managers believe strongly that a crisis is really an *opportunity*. Some companies or products have only come to public awareness in a positive way by promising to make good on something, or by standing behind everything they made, sold, or otherwise guaranteed.

- For decades, Sears, Roebuck & Co. had a reputation for selling good products, but better yet, it had a great customer-service policy, which guaranteed that merchandise could be returned to any store in its chain for a full refund or replacement—in most cases, during the entire life of the product. Many people became loyal customers who described their satisfaction with Sears to others. When the service policy was abandoned to save Sears money, many customers felt cheated. But for years it was what distinguished Sears from other retailers, a fact the company continued to exploit.

- Ford made a successful subcompact car (the Pinto) that was found to have a poorly positioned gas tank, which would explode on even relatively low impact. Ford quickly pulled the model, settled claims quietly, and pointed to its long record of dependable customer service and its extensive charitable and foundation grants. Within a couple of years, the disaster was not only forgotten, but Ford had overtaken GM and the top foreign automakers to have the bestselling car in the United States and much of the world: the Ford Taurus.

- The Tylenol case stands as perhaps the most often-referenced "textbook case" of superb crisis management. The product was tampered with after leaving the plant. Several people ingested tainted capsules and died. The company's parent, Johnson & Johnson's McNeil Laboratories, pulled *all* Tylenol capsules from shelves across the United States, ran nationwide warning ads, and offered replacement products.

The company's CEO bought television time to warn the public of the potential danger and to emphasize personally the company's concern. Most dramatically, he appeared live before an audience of millions of homemakers on a popular daytime television program, taking questions from the audience and by phone from viewers at home. He appeared sincere, concerned, and open. His message was that his company was trusted by millions of people and that the company had an obligation not to let them down. He appeared so sincere—and unusually candid for a CEO—that the public overwhelmingly supported the company, believing the evil person who tampered with the product had made *the company* a victim as well as the unfortunate customers. The brand actually *increased* its market share and remained for years the leader in its category.

In these examples, the companies involved could have suffered insurmountable damage for their problems, which ranged from designing a flawed product to making a product that was easy to tamper with. Yet each company not only survived but came out stronger, in large part by leveraging its reputation and tapping into a long-established reservoir of goodwill. The crises turned into dramatic examples of how a company can put customers' interests ahead of its own profits and do "the right thing," rather than hiding behind walls of lawyers.

Damage control is about maintaining public trust. This is the process recommended to achieve damage control and survive with your reputation intact:

1. Prepare a "situation analysis" in which you identify the crisis, its potential risks, and everyone who will be affected by both the problem and your proposed solutions. Clearly identify your maximum exposure (potential damage).

2. Designate a single spokesperson to announce your position—someone who will be available for follow-up questions and interviews if needed. This person should be media-savvy, well-prepared, and confident. He or she should not project an image of arrogance or other qualities that will compound the problem.

3. Be honest—don't exceed credibility.

4. Go public with your side of the story before someone else does. This will convey a sense of openness and afford you an opportunity to define the situation, rather than responding defensively.

5. *Say something.* Perhaps the worst remark that can be delivered in a crisis situation is "No comment." This is often interpreted by the public as an admission of guilt. Acknowledge that a problem occurred. Then either: (a) tell what you are doing about it; or (b) say, "It would be inappropriate to comment further at this time while we continue to investigate this matter." This conveys the same message as "No comment" but implies thoughtfulness, respect for the questioner, and the possibility that more information will be forthcoming (which likely will have to happen anyway). The ramifications of a crisis can be compounded if it appears you are being uncooperative with those who are trying to explain the issue to your constituency.

6. Plan for a possible "worst-case scenario" and consider how you will handle any situation that might arise.

7. Advertise your position through letters, paid ads, press releases, newsletters, letters to editors, and calls to talk shows.

Point seven essentially summarizes the process by citing the need to publicize your message. As with the company that thought it was enough to post its press release on its website and wait for the world to come looking, nothing will happen to turn a troublesome situation in your favor unless you initiate it. Conversely, a story may circulate *about* you—initiated by a competitor, special-interest group, or someone else who does not have your interests at heart— and then you need to publicize your response to it.

If you perceive or become aware that you, your company, or your product has a bad reputation, consider how that came to be the case: Bad press? A rumor? A lawsuit? Government sanction? Claims by a current or former insider? Some companies that wait for their trouble to simply fade from memory are playing Russian roulette.

Perrier, for example, had some of its bottled water tainted by a chemical at one of its plants. Although the company did express concern and pulled the product from shelves for a time, its response was perceived as tepid—as if it were saying that its public was simply making too much of the matter. When faced with the myriad of choices in bottled water, consumers avoided the risk easily enough by *just choosing another brand*. The market leader's U.S. sales plummeted. Perrier failed to understand that the public had no loyalty to the brand and, in light of the company's attitude, owed it no allegiance whatsoever.

In the aftermath of that crisis, Perrier needed to be more aggressive in both its advertising and its public relations, stressing quality control and product purity. Frequently putting forward a positive image would have served the company better than its strategy of waiting for the story to fade from memory. The interim period of relative inactivity was a time of lost market share. Further, if Perrier had conducted market research, it might have learned that its reputation with the public was not solid enough to help it through such a widely covered crisis.

Public relations can be invaluable, but again, the strategy requires that you don't wait for the public to come to you. There are approaches to getting a message out that "the Technology Age" has made, if not easier, certainly much faster.

One such approach involves placing a bylined article in a trade or general-interest publication or delivering a speech to an industry group. If you plant the article in a print magazine, it could be two to four months before you see it on the newsstands. The process of finding the right industry group and getting the speech delivered could take even longer. By posting the article on your company's or a trade association's website, you can present the material on your date of choice—sooner rather than later. Then, issue press releases announcing the essential newsworthy point of the piece, with aggressive follow-up media calls. This drives home the point regardless of whether anyone goes to the site and actually reads the entire piece. Additional follow-up could include an orchestrated campaign of calls to talk shows, letters to the editor, and participation in Internet chat rooms, which can often generate a significant amount of secondary interest to extend the life of the story.

People Trust Reliable Sources

Consider the number of films, articles, books, and events people know *about* without ever actually seeing or hearing them. This approach has as its premise that, simply put, most people receive most of their information from news coverage or reports, not from actual experience.

If it is a bad idea to post a press release on a website, why is it a good idea to post an article or a speech?

A press release goes to the media (who can be encouraged to use it), whereas an article can be the subject *of* the press release. They are two separate parts of the whole, and good marketing requires that they be handled differently.

If the story is about a person, company, or subject with a bad reputation, is it really wise to extend its shelf life by inviting repeated interest in it?

Yes. If the public perceives a company to have a bad reputation (and such a reputation is unjustified), it may be because the public knows only rumors or reports of negative incidents. Greater exposure to the company will increase awareness, familiarity, and knowledge, and present the subject in a larger context.

People have in fact had their minds changed about a subject and have agreed to revisit the subject, to give it a second try or another look. If Perrier had quickly corrected its problem and announced that an independent testing entity had given it a rating of "pure or better," it could have heavily publicized such a finding (without referring to why it believed it was necessary to do so) well after people had forgotten their lingering concerns over the original incident.

To change a bad reputation, you must generate and disseminate information that tells people positive things they did not know about the subject. It will not happen by passively waiting for people to realize they are wrong.

SUMMARY OF CHAPTER SIX

- Attention begets attention. Media follow the lead of other media in determining much of who and what gets coverage. For this reason, it is naive to assume that a negative story about you, your product, company, or issue will necessarily be forgotten after it appears once in a single report.
- The process of changing a bad reputation involves doing something positive, taking credit for what you do, and publicizing it.

- Damage control is about establishing and maintaining trust. Determine what people think of you; if the image is negative, offer an orchestrated flow of information to present your subject in a larger, more positive context.
- Keeping a low profile may serve a good purpose under normal business conditions. But if a crisis situation arises, it is not advisable that the first thing people know about you is something negative. Damage control should essentially begin *before* a crisis occurs.
- Anticipate a series of "worst-case scenarios" and consider aggressive, high-profile solutions to them. Changing a bad reputation requires that you provide positive information in a consistent, aggressive way. Don't assume that the public or the media will come to you and accept your story on your terms.

editions of specific books, but it has also entered into agreements with a number of manufacturers of clothing, jewelry, and other properties that it determines to be appropriate. It would be fair to suggest that the university has been careful in how and with whom it shares its reputation. The name Harvard (as is true of the short list of other top institutions) adds a veneer of quality, integrity, credibility, and class to products that may not have otherwise had it.

Extending Credibility

Similarly, when a U.S. securities exchange made a definitive statement that specific benefits would accrue to those who invested in its own market instead of other markets, the exchange's remarks were dismissed as self-serving. But when the exchange commissioned two professors—one from the Harvard Business School, the other from Columbia University—to produce a study, the report (which reached the same conclusion) was recognized as scholarly, authoritative, and above suspicion. It was taken for granted that the professors were too highly regarded to compromise their professional reputations for a fee. So what the exchange got for its money was the halo effect of the professors' names attached to a study that would go unchallenged. The same conclusions were advanced both times, but the version that carried far greater weight was the one wrapped in an established reputation.

Good Stock

In that same regard, it is a proud day for a company when it is first listed for trading on the New York Stock Exchange. The company must meet certain requirements and pay a listing fee, but the real distinction is that the company then gets to use the phrase "A New York Stock Exchange–listed company" on all its sales and marketing materials, press releases, business cards, letterheads, and annual reports. Since the NYSE is the preeminent exchange in the United States, its listed companies have been historically regarded as the top tier of actively traded, publicly held businesses.

The prestige and reputation of the exchange is the halo that newly listed companies acquire. Suddenly, they are accorded greater visibility and status among brokers. Consider the fact that many of the same companies' stocks are traded on other exchanges (in Chicago or Philadelphia, for example), but these exchanges are either not referenced at all or designated as simply "other major exchanges." The companies are seeking to identify themselves, for marketing purposes, with the reputation of the market leader.

Designers Practice Reputation Sharing

Perhaps the most lucrative illustrations of the halo effect are found in the area of licensing. In licensing situations, an established brand or designer's name and reputation are attached to a wide range of products that have little, if anything, to do with the original products for which the reputations were earned.

A fashion designer today understands that the value of a name and an image transcends style and even the designs themselves. Even the less successful designers of the fashion industry license their names for use on fragrances, jewelry, cosmetics, luggage, handbags, pens, dishes, glassware, sheets and towels, sunglasses, eyewear, tablecloths, candy, and—in one instance involving a well-known fashion designer—a limited-edition model of a luxury automobile.

Clearly the connection between cars, watches, bedsheets, clothes, and fragrances that carry the same person's name is tenuous at best. What the designer is selling is an image and a reputation that have proven themselves to be worth far more than the actual designs or individual products.

Joan Rivers's reputation evolved from that of an outspoken comedian to an outspoken talk-show host to an outspoken fashion critic on cable TV. Her trademark question to celebrities is "Who are you wearing?" The answer has been worth big dollars. The mention of the designer's name on national television is considered currency: less for the design itself than for the publicity value of linking this designer's name and work to the reputation of someone very famous, whose "look" will perhaps be bought and copied by thousands (maybe millions) of the celebrity's fans. It's the name that interests the audience as much as, or perhaps more than, the dress.

In *Image Marketing*, I wrote:

What Chanel, Dior, Pierre Cardin, and Yves St. Laurent learned to be the case with Paris designers in the seventies is a reality of life for Ralph Lauren, Calvin Klein, and American designers today. It would be unthinkable to successfully introduce a line of clothing without keeping an eye open for what related or unrelated businesses and industries might be developed.

The halo effect can confer status, sometimes even without a specific product. It is the acceptance by a specific audience of an image of something, based on its relationship to something else. In many respects, the halo effect is image marketing at its most effective. When a constituent group feels good about something, it is not unusual for those good feelings to be transferred to something else that's seen as related to it.

Making a Statement People Already Know

The person who wears a class ring, a shirt, or a jacket, or uses a coffee mug with the insignia of his or her college or university is expressing a degree of respect, loyalty, and affection for the institution. But just as importantly, people who do so are overtly trying to associate themselves with their institution's image and reputation.

Companies will often go outside of their own industries, not to mention their product lines, to access the halo effect. One way of doing so is by moving to a particular location, or even acquiring a designation for a current address. For example, First National Bank of Chicago was already regarded as a very prominent local institution, but it still believed that being located at "One First National Plaza" had a somewhat richer sound than just being at the corner of Clark and Madison Streets.

Despite its elegant Park Avenue address in New York, the Metropolitan Life Insurance Company decided "The Met Life Building" would sound better to its customers and investors. While the average company is not in a position to rename a building or a street after itself, companies do find that prestige, or a suggestion of success, spills over to their own reputations if their addresses include words like *United Nations Plaza*, *World Trade Center*, *Park Avenue*, *Fifth Avenue*, *Rodeo Drive*, *Lake Shore Drive*, or even simply "Executive Towers."

Location is the first rule of real estate and retailing, and the place where a company conducts its business has much to do with how people regard it. If the foregoing list of upscale locations seems a bit too much of a move toward style rather than substance, of merely "putting up a false front," please appreciate that for some businesses, location on the high end is extremely important to their reputations: Wall Street law firms, Madison Avenue ad agencies, Paris design houses, Beverly Hills real estate . . .

A company that locates its operations in the garment district, on Printers' Row, in the Mall of America, or in Hershey, Pennsylvania, is using the halo effect to send a message of how it wishes to be perceived. Technology companies exist all over the world, but when a media account makes reference to a Silicon Valley–based company, it suggests a company at the center of the action in the high-tech industry.

Famous Faces, Names, and Reputations for Sale

Moving may not be an option, and the post office is unlikely to redesignate your address as a prestigious *Center*, *Square*, or *Plaza*. So perhaps the shortest route to gaining attention and basking in the reflection of someone else's reputation is the celebrity endorser. Despite the fact that this approach has been overused to the point of being significantly less effective—and nearly a cliche in itself—it remains a tremendously popular approach with companies and businesses at virtually every level, as well as in political campaigns.

When the public sees or hears someone it knows and trusts being identified with you, your product, your company, or your brand, *you* gain trust by extension. For example, take two cars: one is driven by an attractive model, the other by a television personality or sports star. Which car are people more likely to remember? The short answer is *the one with the celebrity*. The slightly longer answer gets a little dicey, since people see so many celebrities in ads that they don't always recall if Tiger Woods was driving a Dodge or a Buick or if Sir Elton John was singing about Diet Coke or Diet Pepsi. Or milk.

But, in terms of the halo effect, identifying a company or brand with a popular or prestigious celebrity figure is generally regarded as a way to buy some image, if not actually any market share.

When Chrysler Corporation was on the brink of bankruptcy, singer Frank Sinatra stepped in to help, filming a commercial for the automaker (for a reported fee of one dollar) in which he and the company's chairman sat down and discussed how important it was that Americans buy American-made products, especially American cars.

Previously, Chrysler had hired former Ford executive Lee Iacocca to head the company. What the company was actually buying was Mr. Iacocca's reputation. He was a nearly legendary figure in the auto industry, credited with successfully launching the Ford Mustang and marketing it to the status of a classic among American cars.

The Sinatra-Iacocca commercial tried to sell cars without ever showing cars or even saying much about the cars themselves. The spot attempted to revive what was perceived as a diminishing sense of patriotism among Americans, particularly among those in the demographic market segment that might be persuaded to buy Chrysler cars. Though the commercial did not run often, it received widespread publicity that benefited the company greatly, as well as adding some luster to Mr. Sinatra's own reputation.

As this case shows, the halo effect is often one of mutual benefit, helping considerably to boost the reputation of the celebrity who's supposedly coming on board to help advance the product or cause. It is as common now for a celebrity to look for a product to endorse, and a cause to support, as it is for a company to seek out a celebrity.

FIGURE 7.1 Sensa

This is a near perfect ad that uses and advances three reputations—those of actor Helen Hunt, the Healing Hands Project of the Healing Hands Foundation, and Sensa pens by Willat. Hunt has offered her endorsement and appears to have signed her photo with a Sensa pen as the brief copy describes how the Project "provides reconstructive facial surgery and loving support to rebuild shattered lives." It is the halo effect, borrowed interest, and reputation marketing at its most effective.

The benefit of this is clear. Reputations are enhanced by association with good causes. The wives of U.S. presidents, who in earlier times were asked to do little more than serve as hostesses at state functions, are now expected to endorse and take on a cause, to do good works and advance their (and their spouses') reputations. Note that Hillary Clinton was a champion of children's rights and a national health care program. Barbara Bush before her was an advocate for literacy, Nancy Reagan led a campaign against drug abuse, Lady Bird Johnson made appearances and speeches on behalf of highway beautification, and Jacqueline Kennedy was an advocate of raising the nation's cultural level and interest in the arts.

It is now simply *assumed* that future First Spouses will embrace causes as a way of making a contribution, as well as using this approach to manage their reputations. Such is the assumed power of celebrity. A "corporate spouse" could similarly identify a cause, work on its behalf, and leverage that association to a publicity advantage in enhancing the reputation of the company.

A company seeking to use its reputation as a marketing device might consider ways in which it can access the halo effect, even if its CEO or spokesperson isn't married to a head of state or constantly photographed with a pop star.

- Has the company, its product, or any of the principals of the organization received an award or other type of recognition?
- Is the product certified as pure or environmentally safe by an accrediting organization whose name or seal would be recognized by the public?
- Have any members of the company or organization's board been recognized for past accomplishments unrelated to the organization: military, sports, politics, the arts, et cetera?
- Is the organization, company, or any member of management prominent in any trade or civic organizations, or serv-

FIGURE 7.2 Milk

The "Got Milk?" ad campaign, in its second decade, could go on indefinitely as long as celebrities, politicians, and likeable everyday people are willing to put their reputations behind the product and campaign that rarely goes beyond thirty-five words of copy. Actor Noah Wyle lends his endorsement and reputation (as well as that of the doctor character he portrays on television) to promote milk's message of nutrition. (Copyright 2000 America's Dairy Farmers and Milk Processors.)

FIGURE 7.3 Cosamin DS

Athletes as paid endorsers may be as old as marketing itself. Baseball Hall of Famer Jim Palmer did well as a spokesman for a loan company and a popular brand of underwear, but his association with a health supplement that is specifically formulated for joints may be the best use yet of his reputation to sell a product. It is a good match, he is believable, and the ad is a no-frills, bulleted list of reasons to buy the product. It may be one of the least sexy, most direct, effective examples of reputation marketing in an ad. (Cosamin DS/Nutramax Laboratories, Inc.)

ing on any charitable or significant boards or committees: United Way, Olympic Committee, tourism group, or a prominent leadership council?

- Does the company or organization have an annual or ongoing charitable effort: food locker, homeless shelter, literacy or scholarship grant, or volunteer organization?
- Has the company or organization invited anyone of particular noteworthiness to serve on its board or in an advisory role?

If the answer to some or all of these questions is no, that situation can be changed with a modest amount of funding, and can help associate the company or organization with a newsworthy entity that will reflect well upon your subject.

Celebrity Executives

Show business has always been a *business*, but the business world is looking a lot more like a show. Financing, recruiting, and presentations to investors are based more and more on the idea of turning CEOs into bankable celebrities and celebrities into CEOs. This is the point at which the corporate reputation, the halo effect, and the celebrity endorser all seem to merge.

Bill Cosby for Jell-O (and Kodak, Ford, and Coke, among others) was a great illustration of "America's Favorite Father," and he used the reflected glow of his reputation to enhance the reputations of products. But increasingly, "celebrities" are coming from the executive suite as well as from the back lot or soundstage:

- Lawyer Johnnie Cochran was able to use his reputation as a visible practicing criminal attorney to become an author and

FIGURE 7.4 Zocor

*General advertising of prescription drugs to the public remains contro-
versial. Since the product cannot be purchased without a doctor's prescription, is general advertising the best use of marketing dollars? Both
sides make persuasive arguments. What then of celebrities being used to
endorse such products? The answer is, only if it is believable. Coach Dan
Reeves suffered heart problems, experienced bypass surgery, and
appears to be a credible spokesman to put his reputation forward to
endorse the cholesterol-lowering drug Zocor. His presence puts a face on
the product, humanizes it, differentiates it from competitors. For those
reasons, it works. (Copyright 1999 Merck & Co., Inc.)*

TV host. Ultimately, he was able to secure financing, recruit legal talent, and generate enormous national media attention for a new law firm with offices across the United States.

- Kurt Andersen's status as a high-profile writer, editor, and bestselling author was enough to make the new startup of the online trade magazine *Inside.com* (and one year later, a companion print version) a well-financed, well-staffed venture. Although the magazine was rich in talent in virtually every department, it was Mr. Andersen's reputation as a "hot" celebrity writer that attracted attention and investors.

It is not uncommon for someone with a track record in a given business to secure funding and publicity for another business. Think of country-music star Jimmy Dean, who became a sausage magnate, and minister Pat Robertson, the head of a media conglomerate. These stars were able to leverage the light of their reputations into business deals.

Political activists; environmentalists; consumer advocates; religious leaders; civil-rights, women's-rights, and gay-rights organizers; and corporate heads of every political and social stripe are regular fixtures on PBS, National Public Radio, C-Span, and dozens of cable news shows. Many have become so well-known as public figures that it has become difficult to distinguish whether *they* are being helped by the halo emitting from their associations and causes, or *the associations and causes* are being aided by their celebrity status. What is clearer is the ability of these people to leverage the strength and radiance of a good reputation into a viable marketing vehicle.

It is extremely common for members of the public to form perceptions of people, products, or companies based solely on their opinions of something else.

Presenting the Halo Effect . . . the Sequel

A product "From the makers of _____ [another product, already established and successful]" has a definable "pre-sell" element that most other products do not have. Publishers, whether marketing their books to a specific target business audience or to the general public, will routinely include the phrase "By the author of _____" below the author's name, identifying the work with a previously well-received product. This is one of the most popular and frequently used illustrations of the halo effect—and of reputation marketing.

The successful introduction of a new extension of an established brand relies totally on the public's knowing the name and reputation of the core product. The marketing effort should need to do little more than mention the core product's name to instantly create a high degree of awareness, recognition, and familiarity on day one.

Personal-care products develop line extensions—a "family of products" built around every successful brand—perhaps including soaps, aftershave lotion, perfumes, colognes, hair dressings, deodorant, shampoo, conditioner. Each is sold separately or packaged together in a stylish designer bag (itself, a line extension).

This is *brand marketing*. If the effort is to be successful, it will incorporate image marketing and exploit the good name (reputation marketing) of the core product, using the halo effect. The basic principles of effective marketing and a few of the marketers' tricks all come together.

Borrowed Interest

Borrowed interest is a strategy that is similar to the halo effect in that it uses an unrelated subject to help you attract attention to your message. Product placements in photographs, movies, and TV programs; at events, meetings, and presentations; and within other products are forms of borrowed interest.

The hotel name displayed on a lectern at a news conference is an example of borrowed interest, in that the hotel is being identified and subtly promoted within a press conference that's about something that most likely has nothing to do with the hotel itself.

Logos are far less subtle than they used to be. The main reason for this is a greater appreciation for promotional possibilities. For generations, golf shirts and sweaters all looked pretty much alike, regardless of their manufacturers. But when the Izod alligator or the Polo horseman began appearing more visibly and identifiably, marketing reached a milestone. Important sports figures were directly or indirectly promoting lines of clothing, watches, or other items that were fashionable and stylish, without even mentioning the products by name. These heroes of the game were pairing their reputations with various corporate identities.

Similarly, when a pop star, a politician, or even an unrecognizable individual is photographed with the Nike swoosh logo prominently visible on his or her shoes, this is certainly an ad for Nike in a non-advertising environment, but it is also a good deal more. The photo might prominently include other items that are important—not so much for the promotional benefit to the products (though they clearly may benefit), but for how the reputation of the person photographed stands to be enhanced. Consider the effect that would be obtained if such a photo were to include an Omega watch, a Mont Blanc pen, a fine work of art (or even a poster of such a work), an expensive musical instrument, a couple of stuffed toys, and an "I Love NY" or Disney World coffee mug. These are all items that very subtly convey an image of the person who owns them—and that image helps create a reputation, upon which a marketing effort can build. They are examples of borrowed interest: using an image or reputation unrelated to you to help convey the image you want to promote.

The Halo Effect and Borrowed Interest as Tools to Change Perceptions

These particular shortcut techniques can sometimes work effortlessly, while at other times they can be employed in a heavy-handed and transparent manner.

The National Rifle Association created a series of print ads using the theme "I am the NRA." In each ad a single individual was profiled, from the likeable and popular TV and film star Tom Selleck to a young, female schoolteacher. The idea was to put a warm, friendly, nonthreatening face on an organization that millions of people perceived to be often militant and militaristic—without dropping the organization's commitment to the ownership of guns.

The organization sought to change its image by presenting its members as the exact opposite of what some perceived them to be. It chose to do this in full-page color ads in *People* and other general-interest publications that reached mainstream America. (This is the same approach *Rolling Stone* magazine used in its long-running "perception versus reality" campaign, in which it attempted to convince advertisers that its readers were not the hippies and flower children they were when the magazine was founded, but grown-up, affluent, educated baby boomers and yuppies.) The concept was solid: to change the negative reputation some people have of a group, show its members in a very positive way.

If there was a flaw in the NRA's strategy, it is that at the same time the "warm and fuzzy" ads were running, spokespeople for the organization were appearing on TV shows and in public debates, presenting the very angry, militant image the group wanted to negate. The lesson for the NRA marketing team (and anyone else in a similar position) is: whichever direction you choose to go, be consistent. Contradictory statements and spokespersons undermine *both* sides of the argument and suggest that the organization is either disorganized or untrustworthy. Neither reputation helps the group's cause.

To take another example, Apple Computer was a sensation when it first entered the market. Its youthful style and spirit of innovation were fueled by the presence of its equally youthful, inventive founder, Steve Jobs. But the company's investors soon worried that the young founder's irreverent, maverick, freewheeling style would not serve the company's longer-term interests as it entered the big leagues. So Mr. Jobs was dumped in favor of John Scully, a serious and thoughtful former Pepsi executive who was brought in to run the company in a more disciplined and businesslike way. It worked for a short time, until Mr. Scully himself was dumped in a period heavy with corporate politics and intrigue and replaced with a now much more matured, subdued, and seemingly disciplined Steve Jobs.

In both of these examples, there is little doubt that a competent manager could have been brought in to run the company or put a serious, businesslike face on the organization. But the high profile of each operation required a high-profile personality and reputation more than it needed a manager.

Caspar Weinberger, President Ronald Reagan's secretary of defense, was not known for his experience in the magazine industry when he was installed as the publisher of *Forbes*. Nor was retired general, later U.S. Secretary of State, Colin Powell asked to serve on the board of directors of America Online because he was known to be particularly proficient at sending E-mail or shopping online. These are two examples of the halo effect, in which efforts are made to enhance a reputation (in these instances, the reputations of both

the companies *and* the individuals involved) and help a company be
all that it can be, by tying its reputation to that of someone else. The
early returns indicate that neither party was hurt, but neither did
the results significantly alter the reputations of anyone involved.
Perhaps in these cases, the shortcut wasn't the solution.

SUMMARY OF CHAPTER SEVEN

- The idea behind the *halo effect* is to bask in the reflected
  glow of an already established, successful entity.
- A connection between core subjects and reflected subjects
  can be direct and obvious, such as a brand extension or
  license, or it can be as subtle as an endorsement from a well-
  known public figure.
- A reputation itself can be a halo effect, as in the case of fashion designers who attach their names and reputations to a
  variety of products, from fragrances and jewelry to restaurants and automobiles.
- It is increasingly common to go outside of one's own industry to access the halo effect, tapping a war hero to join the
  board of a technology company or a well-known retired U.S.
  senator to be a spokesperson for pharmaceutical products.
- Just as location is essential to successful retailing, having "the
  correct address" can help create an image of being well-
  connected, as in *Wall Street* lawyer, *Silicon Valley* software
  developer, *Paris* designer, et cetera.

The Reputation Marketing Casebook

About Companies That Built, Changed, or Exploited Their Reputations

Take no risks with your reputation.
—from a fortune cookie

What do you want to be? How do you want to be known? Some marketers have pulled single words from product reviews and splashed them across the tops of ads, creating instant validation of whatever image or reputation the marketer wanted. To modify the old expression: sometimes a word is worth a thousand pictures. The words on the following list have been used by companies to describe their products, or in some cases, the companies themselves. Consider the images these words bring to mind:

Cool
Hot

Sexy
Wild
Untamed
Wacky
Edgy
Outrageous
Powerful
Earthy

Whether designated as a *positioning statement*, a *slogan*, a *tag line*, or just the main *theme* of a single ad or a marketing campaign, the seemingly simple combination of the right few words has determined winners and losers throughout the years by triggering a feeling about the company or product. Some of the more memorable examples include:

Allstate Insurance Company	You're in good hands with Allstate
American Express	Membership has its privileges
Blackglama furs	What becomes a legend most?
Charmin tissue	Squeezably soft
Clairol	Is it true blondes have more fun?
Coca-Cola	Things go better with Coke It's the Real Thing Coke is it!
DuPont	Better things for better living through chemistry
Forbes **magazine**	Capitalist tool

General Electric	We bring good things to life
Kellogg's Rice Krispies	Snap, crackle, pop
Kentucky Fried Chicken	Finger-lickin' good
Kodak	For the times of your life
Marlboro cigarettes	Come to Marlboro country
Maxwell House coffee	Good to the last drop
McDonald's	You deserve a break today
Memorex audiocassettes	Is it live or is it Memorex?
M&M's candies	The chocolate melts in your mouth, not in your hand
Motel 6	We'll leave the light on for you
Paul Masson wines	We will sell no wine before its time
Rolaids	How do you spell relief?
Sealy mattresses	Like sleeping on a cloud
7UP	The Uncola
Sharp Electronics	From sharp minds come Sharp products
State Farm Insurance	Like a good neighbor, State Farm is there
United Airlines	Come fly the friendly skies
U.S. Army Recruiting	Be all that you can be
U.S. Marine Corps Recruiting	The Marines are looking for a few good men
Virginia Slims cigarettes	You've come a long way, baby
Wheaties	Breakfast of Champions

Clearly this is just a short list—and a highly subjective one at that. Some people would immediately add "The beer that made Milwaukee famous" or "Get a piece of the rock" or "The choice of a new generation." And that's good. More such lines remembered and added to the list is an indication that the creative side of the advertising and marketing mix is doing its job. When a line becomes strongly identified with a company, it is helping to shape and define the image and reputation by which that company will be known, and hopefully, remembered through the ages.

Advertising is a subject about which most people quickly say "I'm no expert," and then just as quickly begin dissecting the latest ads they love or hate:

- Was the ad funny?
- Did you enjoy the music?
- Did you recognize the presenters?
- Was your attention drawn to the minidrama, minimovie, case study, or testimonial; or elements such as a precocious child, beautiful models, bold use of swirling colors, handheld cameras, or cutting-edge artistry?

Those are all questions that agencies and their clients run through as they go down their checklists. For most of the questions, the answer will be *yes*.

But still, most of the ads are forgotten within seconds of being seen or heard. The lines associated with the companies on the foregoing list have remained etched in the minds of at least two generations of consumers because *they created a connection*—a point that spoke of benefit or value to the audience.

Many marketers, feeling an understandable and legitimate need to speak to a new generation, will abandon a classic positioning line in favor of something fresh. Virginia Slims, for example, dropped "You've come a long way, baby," the original tag that had

FIGURE 8.1 Virginia Slims

As controversial as cigarettes are in the marketplace, Virginia Slims is one of the few brands that, by its name-sponsorship of major sports events and its niche of being a "women's cigarette," has maintained a reputation of respectability. Its initial ad slogan, "You've come a long way, baby," was so good and is so identified with the product that people still think of and look for the line in newer ads. More recent offerings, such as "I am not who you think I am. I am who I know I am," fall short with their self-absorbed implications that the original line seemed to dodge. (Copyright Philip Morris Inc. 2000.)

identified the product for decades. Yet when surveyed, respondents still connect that line to the popular cigarette aimed at women. The original line, which ended with a secondary tag, "You've got your own cigarette now," was a perfect way to market a cigarette for women at the beginning of the women's movement in the United States. Later lines, such as "Find your voice," never found their voice. The phrase is a very general reference to individuality; it failed to tie the line to the product.

Apple Computer's interesting "Think different" campaign will not sell a lot of computers, nor will it change the way the market thinks. The full-bleed, black-and-white photographs of famous people, such as Albert Einstein and John Huston, appeared as expensive back-cover ads on mostly upscale magazines, with only the Apple logo and that one awkward phrase as their message. Since Apple users already tend to perceive themselves as creatively and intellectually different than other PC users, the line might be viewed as preaching to the choir. The ads *do* work, however, in reinforcing Apple's reputation for operating outside the mainstream (even if it covets the mainstream sales volume of its less imaginative competitors).

To underscore the impact the right positioning line or slogan can have, consider the companies and lines listed above and try to recall a single ad or commercial for each of these well-known names. The point of this exercise is to show how a company's reputation will be shaped by such a line, which will be remembered long after millions of dollars' worth of media have been dramatically presented and forgotten.

The following case studies examine companies that built reputations in the marketplace. Some of these cases *changed* their reputations; some exploited their reputations wisely; and sadly, some squandered opportunities upon which they might have capitalized.

FIGURE 8.2 Apple Computer

The series of black-and-white photos of dead celebrities under the Apple logo and the words "Think different" want attention for their smugness and grammatical errors. As image ads to maintain Apple's reputation as "ever the outsider" in the technology industry, they do, however, work to reinforce perceptions. (Apple Computer)

■ American Medical Association's Prescription for a Marketing Headache

As trade associations go, the American Medical Association has perhaps one of the strongest franchises in the United States, and—in at least two instances—has given every indication that it's clueless about how to manage it.

From a reputation standpoint, the AMA is blessed and cursed. On the positive side, few professions are as respected, admired, and revered as that of the medical doctor; and few associations are regarded with such awe because of their perceived power and influence as the AMA.

On the negative side, both doctors and their professional association are perceived by many people, at both the highest and lowest levels of society, as arrogant and insensitive.

Some critics have charged over the years that the problem with the AMA is indeed doctors themselves—that healing professionals are not necessarily the best business minds or marketing experts, and may even be incapable of advancing the interests of their profession. Others have claimed that, to the contrary, *nonmedical* professionals guiding the organization reduce the profession to the level of soap companies and (gasp!) salesmen—undignified and contributing to a lessening of prestige.

It is remarkable that the organization has been able to maintain its power and influence, as well as some modicum of dignity, in the face of highly publicized decisions that can only be described, in technical terms, as *really stupid*.

First, consider the concept of the American Medical Association: to promote and maintain the highest standards of professionalism, ethics, and education on behalf of medical doctors. As with any professional association, image and reputation count for a lot. They have a significant bearing on matters of compensation and legislation, both existing and in the future. The organization that represents doctors is clearly important, since—unlike most other professionals—AMA members are called upon to make life-and-death decisions, often quickly and while under enormous pressure.

So it was against this backdrop that the AMA entered into an agreement with Sunbeam Corporation in August 1997. The deal would have permitted the appliance maker to use the AMA seal on its home health-care products. The ensuing protest over this deal—which was regarded at the time as not merely undignified, but a major ethical lapse—resulted in the AMA's backing out.

Adding to the indignity, Sunbeam sued the AMA for breach of contract. The organization paid Sunbeam $9.9 million to settle the matter.

Three years later, with the Sunbeam incident still fresh in the minds of doctors, the media, and much of the public, the AMA board entered into another agreement, this one with the database marketing expert Acxiom Corp. This time the AMA would supply its files on its 650,000 member physicians for marketing purposes, hoping to realize some $19.8 million in exchange.

Much of the AMA membership was outraged, despite recognizing the organization's need to tap whatever potential funding sources it could in order to promote its professional interests and agenda (particularly in the area of legislator lobbying). Many doctors were uncomfortable with the fact that drug companies would have access to information about how many patients received what prescriptions in what amounts.

The AMA defended its move, saying that for physicians to receive marketing information from pharmaceutical companies was actually a very good thing—a way to update doctors on product information in a timely manner. It was also noted that the doctors could "opt out" and advise the companies to stop calling, mailing, and otherwise marketing to them.

Did the AMA commit an ethical lapse?

Yes, it did—if a number of its members, people in the media, and even a small segment of the public *perceived* that it did.

While the AMA may not have *technically* violated any one (or more) of its canons, a professional organization that is responsible for protecting the reputation of its members from even the appearance of impropriety should not *itself* take the organization into questionable territory.

Furthermore, the organization did have other options to raise money (admittedly, perhaps, not as financially remunerative). A membership list of over a half-million physicians is "solid gold" to all who wish to market to this highly prized group. The database does not have to be sold outright in order to make good use of it. Indeed, as a means of protecting members and their own reputations, *most* membership organizations do not grant unqualified access to members' files.

- The organization could have charged a fee to pharmaceutical companies wishing to direct mail to AMA members, under the AMA's supervision. The company provides the contents of the mailing and a fee, and the AMA handles the mailing.
- The AMA could have cosponsored a survey of its physicians that would provide the companies with almost the same type of data that access to its files would have yielded. But this survey would be voluntary on the doctors' part, totally controlled and managed by the AMA, and beyond ethical challenge.

- Pharmaceutical companies could have underwritten the cost of a weekly or monthly newsletter-type vehicle that would provide the company (or companies) a platform for their messages and promotions. The vehicle would direct the physicians to websites, seminars, videotapes, streaming-video presentations, books, and newly published research materials, and provide contacts for those who desire additional information and are inclined to create personal relationships with the companies.

The point is that the first responsibility of the marketing arm of a trade or professional organization should not be to generate revenue, but to provide services to its members. Any time an organization licenses its name, seal, or logo, or grants access to its database, it is relinquishing control of its image, diluting that image, and placing itself in a compromising position.

Physicians have historically and rightfully guarded the reputation of their profession. Such dubious partnerships as the ones noted serve to let down the profession's guard significantly. When such arrangements have to be defended, that's a good indication that they were a bad idea from the start.

Professional associations, regarding themselves as the voice of their industries, too often wait to be asked for information, rather than leading the way in promoting their positions. The AMA should know better. As publisher of *JAMA*—the *Journal of the American Medical Association* (perhaps the most respected publication of its kind), it has a unique and powerful forum from which to speak to its members. The AMA, like other professional associations, must explore the potential of vehicles to carry its message forward to a larger, wider constituency. But it should do so with a dignity that protects its reputation.

■ United States Army

In terms of scope, can there be a greater challenge than changing the image of the United States Army?

The task might seem somewhere between daunting and awesome. Yet, it does provide another excellent example of reputation being "in the eye of the beholder"—how people will see and hear the same characteristics and attributes described and come away with very different perceptions.

To the generation of people who fought or lived during World War II, the thought of the U.S. Army is rich with images of brave, John Wayne–esque, patriotic soldiers who were willing to give their lives for their country.

Baby boomers, on the other hand, took a different view, one that was formed by a different war and a vastly different social and economic climate. The issue of patriotism had largely fallen by the wayside as young people questioned, for the first time as a generation, the correctness and integrity of a cause espoused by the government; accordingly, this prompted them to question the integrity of their leaders.

It is against this backdrop, in a time of cynicism and certainly some confusion and unrest, that the advertising agency for the U.S. Army must tell its side of the story to the *next* generation of potential soldiers.

Recruiting numbers were down, and the Army concluded that it needed a fresh look and sound for its recruiting campaign. So in the year 2001, after an impressive twenty-year run, the Army dropped its enormously successful challenge, "Be all that you can be," in favor of a new campaign built around the theme "An Army of One."

The new idea was meant to appeal to the current target generation's sense of individualism and independence. Market research indicated that young people held a view of the military as "dehumanizing." A new $150 million marketing campaign would correct that.

Maybe.

Or maybe the young people's perceptions were not entirely groundless. Isn't the very concept of an army somewhat dehumanizing, in that it calls upon everyone to sacrifice his or her independence and individualism for the greater good of the cause? Was the Army expecting that prospective recruits would buy into the idea that living together in generic facilities, wearing identical clothing, and pledging adherence to common principles would foster the very description of individualism that the Army was historically identified with *denying*, let alone *encouraging*?

Or was this another gambit likely to set back both the client and the advertising profession, too long identified with tactics such as *bait-and-switch*? Was the Army *not* going to be a tough, driven, demanding, highly disciplined, and structured environment?

Perhaps the research *did* indicate that the "Be all that you can be" campaign had run its course, becoming too familiar and losing its punch. It had, after all, been the only slogan the current target generation of recruits had ever known, predating their birth by at least a couple of years.

But what was truly great about that message was the fact that it urged, asked, and dared each individual to hear it, personalize it, look inside himself or herself and visualize a personal best. It asked the listener to dream big and reach high.

The beauty of that phrase in marketing terms is that, of course, no two individuals would *be* (or would aspire to be) the same thing, giving the phrase a unique personal power. And for purposes of a marketing campaign, it applied to everyone. The phrase is targeted to the individual, yet has the potential to inspire a universe of images.

The U.S. Army, for any number of reasons—including the health of its recruiting program—must focus on its public image and its reputation, both short-term and long-term. It is unlikely that "An Army of One" will be a longer-term campaign, since it does not speak to being part of a team. Instead, it discourages this, and that does not work to the Army's advantage. There were other creative options—a "retro" theme reflecting on the Army's greatest periods of pride and patriotism might have had some appeal to potential recruits, who might have appreciated the concepts of pride, patriotism, and being a part of something important on a global scale.

In the cause of enhancing its reputation, the Army was not, in this case, being all it could have been.

■ The Summer Two Giants Crashed: Ford and Firestone at the Point of No Return

These two automotive-industry superpowers had both been down this dark and winding road before. Ford, one of the world's leading automakers—whose founder's name is synonymous with the automobile itself—had become the laughingstock of the industry when its highly touted new entry into the market, the Ford Edsel, was described by one critic as looking "like an Oldsmobile sucking a lemon." Almost no one wanted to buy the car and it disappeared quickly, but the jokes lingered for years afterward. A generation later, one of Ford's big sellers was the subcompact Ford Pinto, which was a very popular car until it was discovered that through a design flaw that poorly positioned its gas tank, the tank would burst into flames upon even a minor impact.

Firestone, for its part, instituted a major recall of its "500-series" tires in 1978, following discoveries that the product was so flawed that its recall was a matter of life or death.

But neither of these two old, established, well-respected companies had experienced anything like the crisis that engulfed them both in the summer of 2000. Nearly a hundred people were killed while driving Ford vehicles equipped with faulty Firestone tires.

Much has been written about the situation. Public reaction might well be summed up by a letter to *Time* magazine from a North Carolina resident, who concluded:

> The addition of Firestone to the growing list of companies that act as if the lives of American consumers take second place to the bottom line will only further erode the public's trust in business. Witness the ongoing trials of Big Tobacco and your local HMO. Don't these highly paid Ford and Firestone executives get it? If I don't trust a firm's advertising claims, I don't care how good the product is. I will buy from a competitor.

Strong stuff. It wasn't only that Ford and Firestone shared a crisis here, it was, in part, that the two corporate giants seemed to be building to a game of "hot potato" when it came to determining ultimate responsibility for the matter. At first, both tried to downplay the reports of trouble.

In a full-page ad in the *New York Times* and other major papers (the *Times* being especially important, though, as it is among the most often read newspapers by the Wall Street contingent, which has considerable influence over the companies' stock), the president of Ford wrote, "You have my personal guarantee that no one at Ford will rest until every recalled tire is replaced." Separately, a Firestone corporate ad declared, "Our resolution is to regain our customers' confidence and not disappoint them again."

With regard to salvaging two badly dented reputations, it is unlikely that the *deceased* customers will be disappointed with either company in the future. But the rest of the public might have something of a credibility issue with them, as the North Carolina reader of *Time* pointed out.

Public relations has come a long way over the years, and crisis management as an area of specialization has evolved as a particularly disciplined skill. As noted earlier in this book, the most distinguished and often-referenced example of competent crisis management is the Tylenol case—in which, after several deaths resulting from product tampering, Johnson & Johnson ordered a total product recall and raced to reassure the public that safety measures were in place. The company's handling of the situation was applauded, and its CEO won the respect of people who had not previously been Tylenol purchasers. So it was with this experience in mind that the management of Ford and Firestone thought the magic could work again, almost seeming to believe that all they would have to do would be to substitute their names for Tylenol's.

The CEOs of both Ford and Firestone appeared in TV spots remarkably similar to the Johnson & Johnson CEO's ad of nearly two decades earlier. Both gentlemen looked somber and sincere, saying that their respective companies had done much, but were going to work *even harder* because they truly valued their relationships with the public and wanted their trust.

The ads looked fake. It was embarrassingly obvious that the two executives were reading lines written for them by their PR and legal teams—who were evidently urging them to suck up to the public, no matter how embarrassing that might be. What had been, in 1982, a bold and courageous move by a CEO, now seemed like a highly staged, formula performance.

When Firestone had experienced its earlier crisis, it hired actor Jimmy Stewart to appear in TV ads that talked about the company's honorable and distinguished history. That effort proved to be very successful. But another crisis put more than a smear on the company's reputation—it left a skid mark and the smell of burning rubber. In the latest response, both Firestone's print and television ads were famously unconvincing, prompting University of Michigan professor of marketing Tom Kinnear to note, "If you diagrammed how not to react to something like this, Firestone is it."

In *Advertising Age*, Matt Carmichael wrote, "Ford's attempt at damage control packs no punch," adding that the company used various high-profile websites to run an ad that was "simple, classy-looking, almost innocuous. But it might as well say: 'Don't read the coverage by the trusted media site you've come to. Come read it right from us. Our tires might not roll, but boy our PR folks can still spin.'"

Ouch.

Two prominent companies, each a power in their respective industries, both enjoying reputations that had been outstanding for generations, were now being accused of what amounted to gross negligence, and adding insult to injury by mounting damage-control efforts that offered apologies few people, if any, believed were sincere. Some suggested that the damage to the two companies' reputations might be irreparable.

What might they have done differently?

First, the case of Firestone. It would appear that since, in 1978, the Firestone 500s were defective and had to be recalled, and the tires later installed on Ford Explorers and other models were defective and had to be recalled, Firestone had a major credibility problem. Blaming the matter on one particular series or plant would probably not convince the public that the company was being truthful.

Firestone's parent, Bridgestone, might consider retiring the Firestone brand, at least for a period of time—the brand is tarnished, no matter how much the company seeks to reassure people the product is fine. A new name (Bridgestone, Bridgestone II, or something totally new) could be introduced with a high-profile marketing campaign that promises, "Quality control means quality tires." Engaging a prestigious celebrity presenter to deliver a strong, well-crafted message—*without* mentioning the Firestone name—of "a company with a lot of experience and a great track record, with the highest safety standards of any tire in its class," would not be an attempt to *trick* anyone, but would be, in effect, an acknowledgment that the old Firestone company has been remade into a new and better company, which at least deserves a chance to prove its quality and value.

Ford, for its part, should not offer a lame knockoff of the Tylenol damage-control strategy. Instead, it should have a distinguished spokesperson make the rounds of major media (the *Today Show*, *Good Morning America*, *Nightline*, Charlie Rose, National Public Radio). Instead of reading a carefully worded, unconvincing comment from a TelePrompTer or cue card, the spokesperson should sit on the sofa or at the desk with the program's hosts and deliver a sincere statement about how Ford's organization is made up of *people*, who have children and grandchildren who ride in Ford vehicles *safely* every day. The spokesperson should reiterate that the company will not permit any of its employees' children—or anyone else's children—to be put at risk. Then Ford should back it up by promising a "solid-gold safety check," a computer-assisted quality-control safety-check procedure. And make it happen.

It is reasonable to conclude that not all brands can or will last forever. Firestone had a great reputation for decades, but its reputation was tarnished by situations that caused the deaths of innocent people. A very effective crisis-management effort in the past brought forgiveness and another chance. To ask for forgiveness again after still more deaths, and for *yet another* chance, tells the public that Firestone's hopes of salvaging its reputation, its brand equity, and its future profit potential appear to have made the company put its own interests ahead of human lives. This is not a position that invites public support.

Firestone has to restore its credibility with promises that are made good. That will take time. But for decades to come, the Firestone name will be a reminder of faulty products and tragedy every time it is mentioned. The company's best chance for a fresh start would begin with a name that comes without baggage and a product that puts safety and quality first.

Ford has had its share of embarrassments as well, but it has also seen them offset by the Ford Foundation and years of producing numerous models of cars and trucks that appear to be popular and well-made. There is also the fact that hundreds of thousands of Ford vehicles remain on the road, representing a considerable investment on the part of their owners. These people want very much to believe that Ford is a good company with quality products and a genuine concern for its customers. By stressing the company's moral and financial commitment to quality control, the public will likely be inclined to give Ford yet another chance. But the company must realize its position: it is drawing from a reservoir of goodwill that may be close to running dry.

For future companies and marketers who find themselves in similar situations, there is a lesson in the fact that the companies in this case studied successful crisis-management efforts from the past. Their problem was to attempt to replicate the strategy so exactly that it rang insincere to the public. The CEOs of Ford and Firestone were wise to apologize (sort of) and to speak to the public, as the head of Johnson & Johnson did in the Tylenol matter. But they needed to present their own message in their own way—from their own offices or from a newsroom or a lectern, not from a staged and theatrical spot that looked like a thousand other scripted, unconvincing television commercials. The lessons in this for marketers are to (1) be honest in dealing with your public; (2) know your market; (3) know your company and its reputation; (4) determine the extent of the damage done; and (5) fashion a plan to repair the damage, based on your own relationship with your market, not based on a recycled response by someone else to a problem faced nearly two decades earlier.

■ Levi's Jeans—Yesterday's Legend

To many people, blue denim trousers were called *Levi's*, whether that was the brand name or not. Levi's jeans had entered the rarified airspace occupied by a very select few, such as Coke, Kleenex, and Xerox: brand-name products that so dominated their respective categories that their trade names were used freely, as if they were the *generic* names for cola beverages, facial tissues, and photocopied documents. Levi Strauss enjoyed its reputation as the world's preeminent maker of jeans for most of its 147 years in business.

But then, that reputation ended. It appeared an era had ended.

Sales plummeted. The company was forced to close thirty of its fifty-one factories and lay off about 40 percent of its workforce— approximately fifteen thousand employees. When *Business Week* examined the state of the company in the year 2000 and interviewed its new CEO, the resulting article's headline was "Can Levi's Be Cool Again?"

The company's diminishing fortunes were basically blamed on the aging of its core market—baby boomers—and the failure of the company to keep pace with changing styles and therefore appeal to younger market segments. Writer Louise Lee noted, "When fashion shifted to big-pocketed cargo pants, the company hung back— and lost the youth market."

An effort to reach this market with Internet sales was a costly and highly visible failure. Given what the company did and who its customers were, this failure should have come as no surprise.

Levi's CEO outlined what the company would have to do to make a comeback:

- Target kids with hip products such as the casually cut Engineered Jeans, a new Levi's style with large pockets for pagers
- Boost appeal to baby boomers with extensions like Slates casual slacks and Dockers Khakis
- Emphasize products over image in the company's advertising
- Work out glitches in getting products from offshore contract factories to stores. As noted earlier in this book, if problems are not of a marketing nature, they should not be left to marketing to solve. Manufacturing and distribution must *be* competitive to be represented as competitive.

With this as a game plan, chances are very good that Levi's will remain one of the great names *of the past*; its future is very likely to be washed up on some "offshore" shore, where it apparently thinks cheap labor holds the secret to its turnaround strategy.

First, it is important to ask how Levi's acquired its great reputation and maintained it for more than a century. The obvious answer is that it provided a quality product that the public wanted. And, it provided that product at a fair price—or at least a competitive one. "Competitive" means that Levi's pretty much never had the market all to itself, yet the company was still able to maintain its reputation and a healthy share of the market.

So what happened?

A marketer who chooses not to make halfhearted excuses (such as "When the market shifted to big-pocketed cargo pants . . . ")

might simply conclude that Levi's dropped the ball in a major way because it stopped listening to the voice of the market. It obviously gave its customers what they wanted for generations; and then it stopped. That cannot be blamed on the market.

In the same Levi's article, *Business Week* reports, "New ads will showcase the products themselves rather than relentlessly trying to convey 'attitude'." This angle may mean that the company is *still* not listening to the market—or perhaps, anyone else.

Consider how, at the same time Levi's sales are dropping, jeans are highly successful products for Calvin Klein, the Gap, Old Navy, Tommy Hilfiger, Diesel, and a number of other brands, *all* of whom market their jeans with a sense of style and "attitude."

If Levi's believes, as many marketers do, that the product deserves to be the focus of the ad—the argument again of style versus substance—why not have *both*? Emphasize the features that made the product good, better, or best, but wrap it in the kind of sizzling creativity that (1) agencies are paid to provide; and (2) the public will perceive as a message directed *to them* and *for them*, not *for Levi's, from Levi's.*

Additionally, by launching a new line called "Engineered Jeans," Levi's is likely to equal the poor showing Sears experienced when it attempted to sizzle using the boring name "Sears Brand Name Central."

Levi's has such great brand equity and so much on which to build. It could have a campaign that talks to its customers, noting that Levi's is the brand that's always ridden the market throughout the '50s, '60s, '70s, '80s, '90s . . . Levi's could capitalize on the history it has that the competitors do not. If the product is correctly positioned, the company's history will become a supporting message; the primary message should be "Levi's has the jeans you want," or some such pitch that targets both boomers and the younger market.

Levi's needs a strong creative approach and a strong marketing *plan*. The company doesn't need to totally redesign its product lines; it needs to tell the market what's good about its products and why people should care, stressing quality and value as it had done for years. Certainly, it must keep adding new styles (narrower, wider, flared, cargo, farmer-style), just as it had always done.

The market didn't change and move away from Levi's—Levi's hung back and got lazy. As a consequence, it watched its customers choose the companies whose products were talking to the market, having listened to what the market wanted.

After 147 years in business, Levi's management should know that styles and trends come and go . . . and come back again. The company that keeps its advertising fresh and creative, and stays focused on why its product should be the customer's choice, is the product that remains competitively positioned through the years.

A product that can call itself *timeless* cannot blame the market when its time runs out. It just needs to wind up the clock and keep going.

■ The Too-Many Faces of American Express

A company that deals with the public should be concerned about its reputation. One of the industries that should perhaps be most concerned is financial services. The collapse of the U.S. savings-and-loan industry cost investors and the American taxpayers billions of dollars in debts, which aren't expected to be fully absorbed for generations. The roller-coaster stock market and the rise and fall and rise again of mutual funds, options, futures, junk bonds, and index funds have left much of the public understandably wary of the powers that be in banking and finance. And American Express sits at or near the top of the U.S. financial-services-industry pyramid.

At one point, American Express might have laid claim to being one of the best-known, if not *the* best-known, names in the business. Certainly its bank-card competitor Visa saw it as the one to beat, making sure to mention American Express at least once in all of its television commercials.

As has been noted earlier in this book, often the best-known company is perceived to be the *best* company, if only *because* it is the best known. Having left its major credit-card competitors Diners Club and Carte Blanche in the dust, American Express was well on its way to becoming one of the preeminent financial organizations in the world. It purchased brokerage firms (including Shearson Hayden Stone), a respected investment-banking house (Lehman Brothers), a highly successful mutual-fund company (IDS), and led the way in creating credit-card snobbery with its green, blue, gold, and platinum cards that—while not offering appreciably different benefits—carried various levels of cachet.

But then, cracks began appearing in the foundation of American Express. Almost simultaneously, the company schizophrenically engaged in a series of name changes of its acquired companies: branding them as American Express, returning them to their original names, combining the acquired companies in hyphenated marriages, and then back again. It became common to hear questions like "So, is IDS still in business or what?"

American Express also forced many merchants to boycott it for more than a decade in protest of the company's taking a hard line on lowering its transaction fees to merchants, which were higher when compared with other credit or charge cards.

The company rejected an overture from American Airlines to create a co-branded credit card, which would have earned cardholders mileage points with American every time the card was used. Rival United Airlines was enjoying success with a similar program, a co-branded Visa card. When American Express turned it down,

Do you know me?

Probably not. In my business recognition is always important, but when I'm buying goods online I prefer a little privacy. With Private Payments™ from American Express, I get the security of a unique number created for each business transaction I make. It's a safer way to buy because my actual Card number isn't sent out over the Internet. And soon, I'll even be able to control how much information is available about me when I'm surfing the Net, even if it's nothing. Because my private information is my business.

Introducing anonymity online from American Express
Don't leave homepages without it. Enroll at www.americanexpress.com

FIGURE 8.3 American Express

The company effectively brings back its very successful "Do you know me?" campaign to emphasize Internet security and privacy issues. The "masked" face of the customer comes with a touch of irony as the company seems to be in a marketing identity crisis, trying to figure out how it wants to identify with its acquired business lines. Its reputation among some marketers as a flawed giant in the financial services industry could benefit from a more consistent approach. (Copyright 2000 American Express.)

American Airlines took its proposal to Citibank, which enthusiastically accepted the deal and launched the AAdvantage card in both Visa and Mastercard versions. The AAdvantage card became one of the most successful and profitable ventures of its kind.

An embarrassed American Express hastily put together a partnership with Delta Airlines and issued the Delta SkyMiles card, which places distantly behind the American Airlines/Citibank product by virtually any measure.

American Express was still enjoying a high degree of recognition, acceptance, and approval from a public unfamiliar with its corporate stumbles. Actor Karl Malden made famous the company's slogan "The American Express Card—don't leave home without it." Two other ad campaigns—the series of "Do you know me?" ads (featuring people with famous names whose faces are unfamiliar) and "Membership has its privileges"—rank among the best-remembered campaigns of the last quarter-century.

Behind the scenes, however, the industry was abuzz with reports of American Express's continued missteps and squandered opportunities. Customers who fell behind in their payments reported that two American Express companies, Nationwide Credit and G. C. Services, engaged in collection-agency harassment tactics that were reminiscent of another era, complete with late-night abusive phone calls and even calls to the cardholders' neighbors. (One critic of the company, recalling images of mob thugs as "collection agents," suggested that "G. C. Services" stood for "Godfather Collection Services.") This, apparently, was one of the "privileges" American Express didn't mention in its ads.

In 2000, when the company tried selling the idea of privacy protection on American Express customers' Internet purchases, the "Do you know me?" ad campaign was resurrected with the subjects' faces blanked out by computer, prompting some observers to comment that the faces were probably American Express executives who had gone into hiding after their notorious blunders.

How did American Express become so successful? Largely through advertising, and a program of growth by acquisition.

How did its reputation for missed opportunities and harassment of customers go unnoticed by the public for so long? Again, it was the advertising.

A multimillion-dollar campaign featuring entertainment and sports stars, concert and event sponsorships, and highly publicized charitable drives overshadows the tales from the dark side—which have, in fact, been accorded attention in the trade press. (At least two scathing books have been written on the company and its practices.)

To the public at large, American Express is simply known as a very large financial organization. But within its industry, and to outside observers, American Express is a company that greatly needs to sort out what it wants to be. Its five separate status-tiered credit cards (and their corporate-card counterparts) are cannibalizing each other, posing greater competitive threats to each other than they do to Visa, Discover, or Mastercard.

American Express also needs to understand that its prospects for selling snobbery diminished when the 1980s ended and sales of BMWs plummeted. And its hit-and-miss approach to branding its divisions makes the company seem as if it wants credit for the various companies' success *and* the simultaneous ability to distance itself from its less profitable divisions.

Crisis marketers understand the importance of having a single spokesperson. American Express must learn to speak with one voice as a company, and at that, out of only one side of its mouth. The company's interests might be better served by less fragmentation and a streamlining of products. Ten separate credit cards, whose distinction appears largely to consist in their different colors, is not the way to take back lost market share from Visa.

Finally, a company can't claim that "membership has its privileges" and then treat its "members" badly. The division in charge of privilege should be given a course in customer service.

A company that wears one smiling face for the public and another face behind the scenes risks the potential of both faces being seen at the same time. In the end, *integrity* has its privileges.

■ The Gap Came of Age—and It Hurt

Until 1996, the Gap retail-clothing stores had a reputation for selling mostly jeans and T-shirts to teenagers. By all accounts, they did that quite well. But sadly, teenagers tend to undergo a strange metamorphosis and grow up. Often, with a sudden burst, all things teenage are left behind. If you are a retailer, you count on the next group to move into the teenage spot and fill the, uh, gap. For several years this strategy worked out pretty well.

But in a mature moment, the Gap decided not to let go of its aging demographic group without a fight. It launched a second chain of stores—Banana Republic—which offered a more fashionable line of clothing and accessories, and a value-conscious, low-priced chain—Old Navy. Both performed well; and importantly, both reflected a marketing intelligence that made the Gap look very savvy to both customers and investors.

But in 1996, the turning point came as the Gap brand returned to television advertising in a major way, after an absence of some six years. Its memorable campaign, "Khakis Swing," showed a dozen or so twentysomething dancers performing what was called the bop, the jitterbug, or just *swing*, to the song "Jump, Jive an' Wail." The commercial spot used an original 1956 recording of the song by Louis Prima.

FIGURE 8.4 The Gap *The Gap had the reputation of being a clothing store for teens and members of Generation X. TV spots, such as this one featuring big band swing music, appealed to baby boomers as well as younger demographics and helped reposition the company. No dialog or copy in the TV spots sold both the clothes and the image very effectively.*

The khakis looked great with black Gap T-shirts. The young people dancing weren't teenagers, but they also weren't the generation who danced to that record when it was played for the first time to appreciative audiences forty years earlier. The point established by the TV spot—quickly, strongly, and in a most entertaining way— was that the Gap had come of age. Its clothes still turned heads beyond the teen years.

The TV commercial was a huge hit, helping to boost the Gap's image, sales, and stock price. A couple of subsequent campaigns that seemed inspired by the "Khakis Swing" success were entertaining, but progressively weaker.

At the same time, the Gap's Old Navy stores were pushing humor, big value, low prices, and youthful styles, in a very heavy TV ad rotation. Old Navy sales soared as the Gap's sales softened. Gap executives departed the company, citing "creative differences," which observers took to mean they were fired.

By 1999, *Advertising Age* was reporting, "No question, the Gap is coming to grips with the fact that it ain't any longer the only kid on the block," noting in its headline, "With imitators and its own siblings crowding in, retail chain rethinks strategy as another key exec leaves."

The Gap's sales at a fixed point in time may be off from a year earlier to three years earlier when the company was riding the wave of an ad campaign that was highly popular and successful to a degree that most retailers never get to experience at all, much less sustain. But other retailers' sales were off even more during the same period, and the Gap's Old Navy unit was enjoying excellent growth and sales figures that threatened to outshine those of its parent chain—a threat that many investors don't mind being faced with if they are holding Gap, Inc. stock.

Overall, outside the fraternity of number crunchers, the company's reputation is still that of an aggressive, competitive, and often very creative retail chain of contemporary clothing stores. Pressure on the company to add furniture, personal-care products, and intimate apparel could strengthen it horizontally; or, if not managed carefully, the diversification could fracture a well-nurtured image.

The broad messages to marketers in this example are: (1) take the pulse of the market in matters of fashion and respond by giving the public what it wants; (2) tastes can be influenced, shaped, and even changed by a creative presentation of stylish, high-quality products; and (3) don't judge your performance or success on an hour-by-hour basis. If an ad, a campaign, or a product is a total disaster, the message will reach you loudly, clearly, and quickly. But if the fall campaign is not as strong as the previous spring campaign, it is not necessary to fire the ad agency and most of the senior management personnel. It is necessary, however, to make adjustments and keep moving ahead.

Marketers who set unrealistic goals for sales increases—even in soft market cycles—only set themselves and their teams up for a disaster. Business cycles carry companies and industries up and down and back again. A good company with a good product and good message will ride the waves and come through safely.

When the Gap announced, in response to sagging sales, that it would cut back its TV advertising and focus on in-store promotions, the company moved in exactly the *wrong* direction. Sagging sales require *more* external promotion and marketing to drive new customers to the stores while reinforcing your message to satisfied customers. Responding to a downturn by focusing predominantly on customers who are already in the store—and not putting greater energy into attracting the outside market—is another example of preaching to the choir. They love your message, but they are already saved. Good marketing means keeping the message in front of both the customers *and* the prospects, and not panicking if every ad campaign does not win an award.

■ About Sir Richard's Virgin Brand(s)

Certainly, this distinguished and titled gentleman is not the first person to build a reputation solely on a jet-setter personality and flamboyance. Though he might be the first to spread it around like an amazing multinational variety of confetti.

Martha Stewart is regarded as America's most successful "personality conglomerate," having attached her own name to magazines, books, a production company, radio and television ventures, and a very successful Internet site, as well as linens, bath towels, clothing, and a line of house paint. Donald Trump put his name on skyscrapers, hotels, casinos, books, an airline, a board game, and a TV game show—although the last three entries on that list were notable failures.

Sir Richard Branson may be less well-known in the United States than some other moguls and entrepreneurs, but in the United Kingdom his name and reputation are the stuff of legend. A 1998 cover story in *Icon* magazine carried the banner "Richard Branson: Virgin's CEO is a Self-Made Brand."

Indeed. His company Virgin Records has sold millions of CDs by the Rolling Stones, Janet Jackson, and Tina Turner, among other music industry superstars; Virgin Airlines is regarded as a highly aggressive and competitive carrier; Virgin Megastores in major U.S. cities are among the leading retailers of music, videos, books, and electronics equipment; and Virgin Cola is the first serious challenger in a field that Coke and Pepsi had pretty much locked up for years.

In the U.K., however, the list of his Virgin-branded properties and ventures tells an even more dramatic story. Sir Richard holds a majority interest in nearly two hundred businesses, including:

Virgin Active Health Clubs
Virgin Bride

Virgin Cars
Virgin Vie Cosmetics
Virgin Limobike
Virgin Mobile Phones
Virgin Money
Virgin Trains
Virgin Travel
Virgin Wines

There are some three hundred shops in Britain known as V Shops, unique operations that bring all the Virgin online service companies together under one roof.

His autobiography, *Losing My Virginity*, notes that Branson "never misses a beat, sees opportunities everywhere, and is confident enough in his own abilities, and the abilities of those he works with, that he's ready to try almost anything."

Branson believes: "You can learn the nuances of a particular industry in two months."

Some would clearly characterize him as a megalomaniac, and it is unlikely that over the long term, all two hundred of his businesses will be roaring successes.

Could the last 10 Virgin companies have come into being without the first 190? It is hard to argue with the fact that the man has become a billionaire, and has refused to accept a discouraging word.

Throughout Europe, Branson's reputation borders on legendary. While still in high school, he began publishing a magazine that he described as "an alternative magazine with a fresh attitude." The magazine, called *Student*, was distributed throughout English private schools. Though it was political in its focus, Branson managed to convince Mick Jagger, John Lennon, and Vanessa Redgrave to be interviewed.

Branson seems to view the establishment of one venture as a way to widen the platform for another. This is in contrast to the more common corporate mentality that has companies becoming more conservative and cautious as they become larger and more sensitive about their accountability to boards of directors and investors. Branson flaunts the fact that he takes risks. He projects a high profile and a highly confident presence as the spokesperson for his ventures, and it seems that his enthusiasm inspires the public to at least want to try his various products and companies' services.

Red Herring reported that "Mr. Branson doesn't see the incongruity in an airline, cosmetic company, and a car dealership all being lumped under the same brand name. Instead, he sees beauty in brand leveraging."

Branson notes, "I think you can stretch a brand as long as you stretch it with quality and you offer good value and you do it in a way that is different from other people."

Radical? Eccentric? Highly unbusinesslike for a serious businessperson?

Perhaps. But few would dispute that the energy, enthusiasm, and confidence this risk-taker brings to his ventures has taken him far. In terms of reputation marketing, Branson serves as a reminder that investors and the public like to back a winner. Risk-taker though he may be, he has leveraged his reputation horizontally to create so many companies (on the chance that more of them will succeed than will fail) that it only takes a few *megasuccesses* to generate enough light to outshine those ventures that don't pan out. Viewed from that perspective, the high-risk approach almost seems like an insurance policy. It may not be right for everyone, but it has taken Sir Richard Branson and his hundreds of Virgins a long way since high school.

■ For Arthur Andersen, Andersen, and Accenture, It Is as Difficult as 1-2-3

The Big Eight accounting firms became the Big Five. Or should that be Six? Don't ask your consultant, because he or she is packing to leave and move across the street to operate under a new name—or perhaps under the same name, although the company will be completely different—but it's not to be confused with the successor company, which will do exactly the same thing.

Sound confusing?

It is. Especially coming, as it does, from the accounting firm that is supposed to take a look at the company and reassure investors that everything checks out fine. You can trust them, whoever they are. Probably.

The foregoing was not an addendum to the tea-party scene in *Alice in Wonderland*. It is how a number of marketers (not to mention investors) reacted to the evolution—or devolution—of Arthur Andersen, one of the world's largest and most successful accounting firms. While competitors KPMG and PricewaterhouseCoopers consolidated their respective operations as the merged entities that lead the shrinking ranks of preeminent accounting firms, Andersen went its own way until a very public, very messy divorce of the firms' accounting partners and its consulting operation. The consultants then announced they would be hanging out a new shingle that read "Accenture."

While the debate continued concerning how well the now-differentiated companies would do after parting, Andersen (the accounting partners) prevailed in a dispute with the Securities and Exchange Commission, which was seeking to limit its lines of business to prevent possible conflicts of interest. With that battle behind them and their consulting operations now moved on, Andersen (the accounting partners) announced that they would establish a consulting business.

After we take a couple of extra-strength pain relievers for the headache that commonly accompanies such explanations, let us examine the reputations of—and marketing implications for—this intense group of once and future family members and competitors.

For decades, Arthur Andersen maintained its reputation as one of the world's most prestigious accounting firms, its impressive list of blue-chip clients serving to attract even more blue-chip clients around the world. Despite governmental concerns about a possible conflict of interests, Arthur Andersen established Andersen Consulting, a business unit that acted as advisor to companies that the firm audited. Arthur Andersen insisted that having a separate group of professionals in accounting and consulting roles would ensure complete integrity and not compromise the firm's role as auditor of the clients it served.

The consulting practice proved to be extremely lucrative—so much so that the consultants quickly became resentful of what they perceived to be an imbalance in ratios of earnings to compensation. That is to say, the consultants balked over the fact that they were generating more revenue for the firm than the accountants were. The accountants were profiting handsomely and (the consultants believed) disproportionately.

After a six-year period of high-profile public acrimony, the consulting division broke away from Arthur Andersen and formed Accenture, an international practice of some sixty-five thousand consultants.

Arthur Andersen's CEO sought to downplay the matter by saying, "We were partners previously with people who did not want to be our partners." Noting that the field was too fertile to abandon and indicating an intention to rebuild, he added, "At least half of our firm does one kind of consulting or another. It will grow very quickly."

So the huge worldwide firm that was Arthur Andersen, with so many different operations doing business under numerous variations on the Andersen name that many *employees* had difficulty sorting it all out, became an accounting firm without a consulting practice. (It is still determined to rebuild that capability, despite the expressed desires of its big accountant competitors, sensitive to concerns about potential conflicts of interest, to divest themselves of their consulting practices.)

The fallout from the prolonged public bickering proved to be not so much a tarnished reputation as simply a great deal of confusion. Normally, such family feuds turn off both clients and the public, but in this case, Andersen had two things going for it: (1) a public accustomed to witnessing very open breakups; and (2) its status as a large global operation that provides quality services, which are so valued by clients that they appear willing to put up with a great deal.

Arthur Andersen now presses on, viewed as having more of a pronounced limp than the major dismemberment it might have experienced. From the executive suite, Andersen's management projects such supreme confidence that clients indeed seem to be reassured. It might also be concluded that the shrinking number of firms in the profession has permitted a "reshuffling" of top organizations to occur, rather than the usual competitive intensity typical of a more crowded field.

As for the cut-loose firm that became Accenture, it launched a costly corporate-identity advertising campaign to tell the world of its existence, if not its back story. Its ads included the line "Formerly Andersen Consulting," without noting that there was no longer a connection to anything Andersen.

Most corporate-identity experts agree that calling itself Accenture—a created word with no history—may prove to be the consultancy's first major misstep. The public likes to hear words it knows and understands. When the former head of United Airlines changed the parent holding company's name to Allegis, the marketplace reacted with a groan and noted that considerable brand equity had been disregarded. Soon the Allegis name was dropped and the company was rechristened UAL, Inc.

Accenture may have been part of something else, but as a new company it needs to establish its own reputation. Choosing a name without meaning only makes that task harder, although its ad budget of over $100 million will help. It is worth considering, however, how much easier Accenture could have made its task.

Whether it's involved with accounting or consulting, Andersen, like General Motors and Ford, will be able to withstand many hits before it shows major damage. Management, however, should remember that the firm is less resilient than a cat; it won't be allowed to lose nine lives before the market decides it is truly dead.

During the infighting, neither side seemed to put much energy toward maintaining its reputation. Andersen was seemingly so well capitalized that it assumed its flag would forever wave. And the breakaway consultants were pleased to have clients and business.

A good reputation is critical in the consulting/management profession. All sides should understand that clients come and go, but a reputation is something that stays, for better or worse.

■ Philip Morris, Kraft, Taco Bell . . . Recalls and Other Snapshots in Reputation Marketing

In years past, the recalls of cars, prescription drugs, over-the-counter remedies, toys, and other items identified as potentially hazardous were headline stories that rocked entire industries—and on occasion, the stock market as well. The power and prestige associated with so many corporate reputations, and the public's diminishing trust and respect for the media that have often inflated and sensationalized stories, have combined to make the public more suspicious and sometimes indifferent to the news of a recall. For marketers, this is good news and bad news.

The bad news is that the challenge becomes even greater to impress, persuade, and sell to a public that is increasingly jaded and inclined not to believe what an ad presents as fact.

The good news is that a well-informed, thoughtful, and discriminating public does not panic and sink a long-respected company or product because of a story that may not have received fair or objective coverage.

Tires were not the only notable product recall in 2000. Scooters made a comeback for a time as the year's most wanted toy, replacing skateboards and in-line skates, until the product's safety was called into question after reports of hundreds of emergency-room visits that resulted from scooter-related accidents. Thousands of scooters were recalled, the result of defects in design and construction.

But perhaps one of the most interesting and unusual recalls of that dubious year was that of the nearly 2.5 million boxes of taco shells marketed under the Taco Bell brand name and manufactured by Kraft Foods. The U.S. nationwide recall began after Kraft confirmed that the product contained a genetically engineered type of corn that had not been approved for human consumption by the Food and Drug Administration. The corn was approved for animal feed only.

The first announcement of the nonapproved corn came from Genetically Engineered Food Alert, an environmental- and consumer-group coalition that is critical of the process of creating bioengineered food. A trade group that represented the biotechnology industry challenged the coalition's product test by way of response, and just as the matter was beginning to look as if it would escalate into a major public-health debate, Kraft confirmed the coalition's test and ordered the recall.

The story was deemed newsworthy for just a couple of days, or what the industry regards as one news cycle. Little has been heard about it since. Kraft, after all, is one of the world's largest food and food-product marketers. But it is also criticized on regular occasions for the manufacturing and mass marketing of items labeled "food products" that have little or no nutritional value.

This incident could have set the stage for a major attack on Kraft as well as on its parent company, Philip Morris, which, as one of the world's largest producers of tobacco products, is always vulnerable to attacks. Philip Morris has often been criticized for purchasing large, established nontobacco companies such as Kraft, as a means of wrapping itself in a more respectable, less controversial corporate image.

And of course Taco Bell was a ready target for criticism for having licensed its name to a company that produced supermarket products; if the taco shells were determined to be truly harmful, this could taint the reputation of the entire chain of fast-food restaurants—restaurants that operated scandal-free before (perhaps unwisely) forming this relationship.

Despite the fact that the fuse burned without the explosion ever occurring, how did three such highly visible companies, one a more likely target for special-interest-group attacks than the others, escape the brush of a scandal wide enough to tar them all?

Perhaps more than anything else, the reputation of Kraft Foods saved the day. Its nutritional issues notwithstanding, Kraft produces hundreds of products that have resided on consumer

been doing its good work for longer than Philip Morris appears to have been writing checks for them.

In a separate ad that is part of the same campaign, the headline reads, "Jared had the grades and the determination. Now he's got the tuition, too." In this ad, of less than eighty words of copy, Philip Morris is again mentioned five times (plus the logo). And again, the company's role is as a contributor, in this instance to the Thurgood Marshall Scholarship Fund and "over 350 other educational organizations that help strengthen local communities."

The TV spots in this campaign follow the look and tone of the print ads.

Hunger programs and scholarship programs rely on corporate generosity for their funding, and Philip Morris should be commended for its generous tax-deductible contributions of cash and products. But wouldn't it have been a nice touch to add the cost of this ad campaign to the actual donations? An educated guess as to the campaign's cost might reasonably be $100 million or more.

Advertising is an effective and honorable means of delivering a corporate message. It is to be encouraged. However, for a company with profits in the billions of dollars, which agrees to a settlement of a government-initiated lawsuit in which it will pay several more billion dollars, the tactic of spending millions more to tell the public it is perhaps more noble and virtuous than they might have suspected is—at its best—highly transparent.

If Philip Morris were to actually create worthwhile programs, and implement them with a paid staff and volunteers from within its companies, the company might deserve more credit than it gets from simply writing the checks to the selfless people who do commit themselves to helping others.

And if the same ads were to not even mention Philip Morris, but instead focus more on Meals on Wheels, the Thurgood Marshall

FIGURE 8.5A The Philip Morris Companies

This is a bad time to be known as a tobacco company (albeit an extremely profitable one). Diversification, particularly in the area of food companies, appears to take some of the edge off the situation. A high-profile campaign to provide food for senior citizens (A) and funding for education (B) seems like a good idea, unless it appears overtly self-serving and raises questions about the true intentions of the company—as this campaign does. Changing the unfavorable reputation of tobacco companies, as viewed by much of the public, requires more subtlety than the Philip Morris Companies employed in this campaign. (Copyright 2000 Philip Morris Companies Inc.)

Jared had the grades and the determination. Now he's got the tuition, too.

Thanks to Philip Morris' contributions to the Thurgood Marshall Scholarship Fund, honor student Jared Reaves got a full 4-year scholarship. For the last 13 years, the Philip Morris family of companies has been the Fund's largest donor, helping thousands of deserving students get the opportunity they've earned. Philip Morris also supports over 350 other educational organizations that help strengthen local communities. For the whole story, visit philipmorris.com. Working to make a difference.

THE PHILIP MORRIS FAMILY OF COMPANIES

KRAFT PHILIP MORRIS U.S.A. Miller

FIGURE 8.5B **The Philip Morris Companies**

Scholarship Fund, and other worthy programs, thereby encouraging readers and viewers of the ads to volunteer or contribute to these causes themselves, the ads' contribution would be so much greater.

What about giving credit where credit is due?

It might be done in a variety of ways. One approach might be to sign the ad "A message from the PM Foundation," followed by a small (modest, humble) mention that the foundation is funded by the Philip Morris Companies as a service to the community.

Another approach could be a one- or two-year funding of the campaign with *no* attempt to be recognized, and then have the CEO identify the company as the generous benefactor in its annual report, which its PR people would be sure to provide to the media. Such humility and generosity would not go unnoticed, and would serve to benefit the company much more than future multibillion-dollar plea bargains.

Cause marketing is an excellent way to practice reputation marketing, but when the demand to be recognized so outshines the generosity of the act as it does in this example, the whole point— and advantage—of the effort is negated. The best marketing programs require skill, creativity, and a certain degree of subtlety. A program that beats the audience over the head with its message leaves the audience with a headache.

■ This Section Sucks: Villains in Cyberspace

At first glance, the following "cybertactics" look like a joke, or perhaps someone's attempt at mischief, but a closer look shows they are anything but harmless.

Once upon a time, a name followed by the word *sucks* spray-painted on a wall was the height of insult, if not obscenity. Times change. The word *sucks* has evolved in its everyday usage to mean little more than what used to be associated with a word such as *stinks*. While it is certainly no compliment, to say that something sucks is simply to dismiss it, with an increasingly hollow and empty reference.

That may be changing.

Cybertechnology has brought new life to many businesses and industries, but it may also be reversing the old proverb: names may soon be able to hurt people even more than sticks and stones.

The problem started with the practice of "cybersquatting," in which someone would register the domain names (the URLs) of celebrities and major products and businesses *before* the actual bearers of those names got around to doing so. Then the cyber-squatter, who might hold a huge number of registrations, would attempt to sell the registrations to the individuals and companies that might have a justifiable interest in owning them. For example, if the actress Julia Roberts wanted to own the URL "Julia Roberts.com", she would have to buy it from a cybersquatter who had registered it ahead of her.

An enterprising pornographer took the process even further by registering the names of numerous businesses, brands, and individuals with the words *sucks.com* after each of them. Although the term has largely developed into a simple disparaging reference, when used to create a website it carries the potential to rally critics, disgruntled current and former employees, and special-interest groups opposed to a subject, at a single location that can serve as both a sounding board for negative expression and a source of bad publicity in and of itself.

Lockheed Martin, the giant aircraft company, sued to gain control of a cybersquatter's registration of Lockheedsucks.com.

The group PETA (People for the Ethical Treatment of Animals), known for routinely employing "in-your-face" tactics to register its point, attacked milk producers with a parody of the popular "Got Milk?" advertising campaign. PETA sponsored billboards showing New York's mayor, Rudy Giuliani (who has prostate cancer), with a painted-on white mustache and a headline that read "Got Cancer?" This was followed by the website address www.milk-sucks.com.

In bad taste? Sure.

Hard-hitting enough to achieve its objective of getting noticed, shocking people, and being talked about? Definitely.

But it wasn't just the edgy headline and the strong visual, it was the website and the invitation to follow up, not at PETA.com or cancerinfo.com, but at milksucks.com. And the URL was legally registered.

To return to the earlier example, a Lockheed company spokesman said, "Our policy is to take actions necessary to protect our good name and brand equity."

Fair enough. Lockheed is a well-heeled company that very likely anticipates some lawsuits, a degree of bad press, and probably a scathing editorial or syndicated column from time to time. But a Lockheedsucks.com *website* suggests the existence of an organized, ongoing burr in the saddle of the company—an electronic chain letter, a bulletin board, or a town meeting—that costs the company's critics very little, while costing the company itself a considerable amount to effect a counterbalance. The website might serve as an open invitation to reporters, commentators, and others in need of an issue *du jour*.

In the past, muckrakers would have to sniff around for months, or even longer, to find a former employee or an unhappy customer with a complaint, grievance, or documented bad experience. Today, one need only point and click, and the Internet will lead you to someone with a story to tell.

So, how does a company that has labored long and carefully to create and preserve its reputation bring itself to engage in such guerrilla tactics and do battle in cyberspace?

The best, most effective strikes are always the preemptive ones. Consider using your own website *and* a traditional printed newsletter, as both a preemptive and a response mechanism. Devote a section in both your website and newsletter to answering real or anticipated complaints and criticism, whether they come from employees, shareholders, or the media. (If the subject matter is hot enough, issue a press release defining the subject on your terms; that way you can address it early, rather than defensively responding after the fact.) Also, in the same electronic and print vehicles, create a "lighter side" section, in which you approach a subject with humor, perhaps even poke a bit of fun at management.

This show of good humor and willingness to not take yourself too seriously (except in the most serious matters of business) helps position you for digs and cheap shots (the "sucks" matter, for example). It makes critics' attacks seem even more mean-spirited and unworthy against your backdrop of openness and goodwill.

Just as a crisis-management plan is a good tool to have available just in case it's needed, taking the initiative to get yourself out in front of your critics is a way to keep *you* in control of your agenda.

SUMMARY OF CHAPTER EIGHT

- Successful companies have helped to advance their reputations by establishing a particular imagery that defines the companies in their advertising and marketing programs. Often such words as *outrageous, sexy, cool, wild, wacky, untamed,* or *edgy* will characterize such ads or allusions.
- Companies that try to build awareness and a reputation with humorous or shocking ads should first consider the sensitivities and tolerance levels of the public or demographic tar-

get group and second, determine if such an approach is consistent over the longer term with the reputation or image that is desired.

- In an effort to generate revenue, companies will license use of their names or logos to products or other companies, which then become, in effect, an endorsement of the licensee. It is important to consider if such an arrangement will diminish a reputation (as happened when the American Medical Association allowed its seal to be used on Sunbeam products).

- When an ad campaign or theme helps to create a strong positive image, the follow-up campaign should reinforce that image. In some cases the sequel campaign can redirect or reposition the subject and the result can diminish the subject's overall reputation (as was the case when the U.S. Army replaced a twenty-year-old ad campaign with a notably weaker campaign).

- Generations of accumulated goodwill may need to be tapped in times of crisis. At such times it is crucial to be honest and not to compromise a reputation by ducking responsibility for a problem (as Ford and Firestone did in response to charges regarding the quality of their respective products).

- A company that is a market leader must remember what it did to earn that reputation and not respond to declining market share by ignoring the voice of the market in apparently desperate attempts to appear new again (such as the case of Levi's jeans).

- Show appreciation for being a customer's brand of choice. A company that builds its reputation on providing service to its customers and offering status and privilege shoots its reputation in the corporate foot by maintaining policies that then offend, insult, and confuse (as happened with American Express).

- Creating too many brand extensions or spin-offs can confuse the marketplace and devalue a good reputation.
- Transparent, self-serving ads and programs in which a company congratulates itself for supporting good causes in the community can backfire and leave a company's questionable reputation in an even worse condition.

CHAPTER NINE

A Crash Course in Reputation Marketing

Following is a quick summary of what you need to keep in mind to be successful in your reputation marketing campaign.

- Be honest with your employees, your customers or clients, your shareholders, and your regulators, but most of all with *yourself*. Use market research to validate what you think you know about your reputation and to tell you things you don't know.
- Beware of people who tell you what their reputation is. Usually, they are telling you *their perception* of their reputation. Someone who says "I'm very good at what I do," or "I have

a reputation for excellence," is not the most objective source for such information, nor does such a statement usually reflect conclusive data to that effect.

In reputation marketing, it is a good idea to check your ego at the door. We've all heard of an executive who entered a crowded meeting room and announced, "Most of you are familiar with my company, right?" Very few people were. Managing your reputation requires a degree of objectivity.

- Success is not the same thing (nor should it be interpreted) as a good reputation.
- Being profitable is not the same as having a good reputation.
- Being well-known is not the same as having a good reputation. Many well-known people and companies are not well liked (and may even be *disliked*) but are the only available choice. This is true of some telephone companies, cable companies, the only newspaper in town, and so on. This status should be viewed as an opportunity to win support. To be indifferent to a bad reputation is to willingly place yourself in a vulnerable position and to acquire a constituency that would welcome your falling upon difficult times.
- Draw distinctions between celebrity, notoriety, and a reputation. Think of a business's reputation as how people come to regard the business over time, rather than what they think at a fixed moment. For example, a company that strives to be known for creativity and high energy—a "hot" company— will crank up its publicity efforts, planting stories about its activities anywhere and everywhere, from online newsletters and chat rooms to quarterly journals and call-in shows. These businesses often do in fact get noticed—and frequently labeled opportunistic publicity hounds. They get a reputation for focusing a disproportionate amount of energy on *getting*, rather than *earning*, a reputation. And the sub-

stance of the reputation they get is dust, stirred up by activity rather than by accomplishment.

- Politicians are among those who think of their reputations as a legacy, as the way they will be regarded by history. They attempt to control events that promote appearances and an image of style rather than substance. Historians check the record of the times, but seek to attribute *motivations* for actions as well as the actions themselves. If indications are that events and news were managed more for image enhancement than for worthwhile purposes, the resulting reputation will indeed be a legacy—though not the reputation that was sought. Similarly, a business or corporation that promotes its involvement with causes or other good works *just for publicity purposes* will lose, rather than gain, the public's goodwill.

- Reputation marketing treats the public's positive perceptions of a subject, company, brand, product, or cause as an asset to be shaped, nurtured, protected, and used to advantage.

- A good reputation-marketing strategy encourages giving something back to the community, whether as a volunteer or as the underwriter of a worthwhile service or educational effort.

- Research is more than information. It can in itself be a valuable asset that can be put to work. Learning what people think of a company can provide selling points or other opportunities for exploitation.

- Understand what your target market thinks are important points to know about you. For example: quality, value, price, service, and guarantees might be obvious selling points. To a young audience, the number of years a company has been in business may be totally unimportant. But in the matter of a professional-services business (lawyers, doctors, accountants, pilots), experience may be extremely important. Often, *what* a company or service provider has done will be regarded as more important than how long they've been doing it. Know what your market wants to know about you and plan accordingly.

- Your name and reputation are linked. It is not only important that your name should stand for something, but that people know what your name means. Acronyms and clever made-up names are inside jokes. Tell people who you are by choosing a good, business-related name.

- Be aware of the sensitivity of your market. Offending people is not good for your reputation, nor is it good marketing. If your target audience is young, market to that audience, but not in such a way that is troubling to older (or other) market segments. Upsetting or excluding any market segment is not good marketing.

- Be out front and active. Marketing is never about waiting for the phone to ring. Whether online or on-site, you should advertise, mount a PR effort, sponsor events or programs, and bring your message to the marketplace. *That* you do it and *how* you do it will define your reputation.

- Changing a bad reputation into a good reputation is not simply about being right and waiting for people to realize it. Changing a reputation requires doing positive things and consistently presenting a positive story on a frequent basis.

- Good damage control is a matter of earning trust, maintaining trust, and receiving credit for the good you do. Keeping a low profile is less expensive than maintaining an advertising and public-relations program, but if a crisis or negative story should appear, the first news the public receives about you should not be bad news. Creating an image or reputation may be difficult and take time, but *changing* a bad reputation to a good one is even more difficult.

- A reputation can derive from *borrowed interest* or the *halo effect*—basically, benefiting from an association with someone or something people like, respect, or appreciate.
- A business address can be used for reputation marketing. *Where you are* can, in some instances, influence an opinion as much as *what you do*: for example, as in *New York* agent, *Paris* designer, or *Wall Street* lawyer.

In a single season, Firestone, Ford, and United Airlines bought television time and print space in order to apologize to the public; Royal Dutch/Shell abandoned plans for a North Sea oil rig that environmentalists said was contaminated; Archer Daniels Midland pleaded guilty to a price-fixing conspiracy that cost consumers millions of dollars (the company agreed to pay a $100 million fine); and Merrill Lynch was reported to have helped its corporate clients set up shell corporations to create a tax dodge.

These are examples of ethical lapses and an insensitivity to public concern that threatened to undo decades of excellent service and integrity, and provided competitors with a chance to exploit these lapses and increase their own market share at the expense of the companies named. All the contributions, grants, goodwill efforts, and relationships became vulnerable.

A reputation is an asset that can help a marketing program. Consider what comes to mind simply at the mention of a title: *Doctor, General, Judge, Professor, Reverend, Senator, Counselor* . . .

Think of the imagery when someone says *feminist, teenager, senior citizen, hippie, environmentalist, activist, reformer* . . .

Appreciate the importance to a business or cause that a simple "label" can provide. A good image and a good reputation can help marketers achieve more, faster, for less. To start, tell your friends about it.

Bibliography

Advertising Age: "CEOs' summer fashion—the hair shirt" by Mercedes Cardona, September 4, 2000; "Cyber critique" by Matt Carmichael, September 18, 2000; "Firestone's dilemma: Can this brand be saved?" by Jean Halliday, September 4, 2000; "Marketers of the Century" by Jack Neff, Louise Kramer, Wayne Kramer, and Wayne Friedman, December 13, 1999; "McMakeover" by Kate MacArthur, July 17, 2000; "Nasser spot lacks star quality" by Bob Garfield, August 28, 2000.

The Brand Marketing Book: Creating, Managing, and Extending the Value of Your Brand by Joe Marconi. Lincolnwood, Ill.: NTC Business Books, 2000.

B to B: "Andersen becomes Accenture" by Philip B. Clark, November 6, 2000.

Business Week: "Can Levi's Be Cool Again?" by Louise Lee, March 13, 2000; "Now Coke is No Longer It" by Dean Foust with Deborah Rubin, February 28, 2000.

Chicago Tribune Business: "Arthur Andersen marches ahead in the consulting arena" by Robert Manor, January 21, 2001; "Good Bobby, Bad Bobby," a book review by Todd Gitlin, September 24, 2000.

Crain's Chicago Business: "AMA Blasts Crain's Coverage of Marketing Venture" letter, December 4, 2000; "AMA deal under fire" by Sarah A. Klein, November 13, 2000; "AMA's son-of-Sunbeam deal damages credibility" editorial, November 20, 2000; "Dot.com allure is fleeting for many" by Ed Avis, November 27, 2000.

Crisis Marketing by Joe Marconi. Lincolnwood, Ill.: NTC Business Books, 1997.

Guerrilla Web Strategies by Vince Gelormine. Scottsdale, Ariz.: Cariolis Group Books, 1996.

Hearing the Voice of the Market by Vincent P. Barabba and Gerald Zaltman. Boston, Mass.: Harvard Business School Press, 1991.

Icon Magazine: Richard Branson profile by Morgan Strong, December 1998.

Image Marketing by Joe Marconi. Lincolnwood, Ill.: NTC Business Books, 1996.

New York Times: "Ads Now Seek Recruits for 'An Army of One'" by James Dao, January 12, 2001; "Ford and Firestone Settle High-Profile Suit Over Explorer Crash" by Michael Winerip, January 9, 2001; "Getting Religion on Corporate Ethics" by Amy Zipkin, October 18, 2000; "Kraft Recalls Taco Shells with Bioengineered Corn" by Andrew Pollock, September 23, 2000; "A Year Underachievers Can Be Proud Of" by Gretchen Morganson, December 31, 2000.

Red Herring: "Sir Richard aims his branding lance aggressively at the U.S. market" by Gentry Lane, September 2000.

Time: Letter to the editor regarding "The Road to Recall," October 2, 2000.

USA Today: "Profiteers get squat for Web names" by Jon Swartz, August 25, 2000.

Value-Added Public Relations by Thomas L. Harris. Lincolnwood, Ill.: NTC Business Books, 1998.

Wall Street Journal: "How the Rubber Meets the Road" by Robert Guy Matthews, September 8, 2000.

Index

About the Author

Joe Marconi is a marketing communications consultant and writer with more than two decades of award-winning advertising, public relations, and marketing experience. He is the author of nine books including: *The Brand Marketing Book*, *Image Marketing*, *Crisis Marketing*, *The Complete Guide to Publicity*, and *Future Marketing*. His newsletter, *Marconi on Marketing*, is published online at www.Marconi-on-Marketing.com. He lives in Western Springs, Illinois, near Chicago.

You can contact him at:

Joe Marconi Marketing Communications, Inc.
Phone: 708/246-7102
Fax: 708/246-6790
E-mail: JAMarconi@aol.com

The American Marketing Association is the world's largest and most comprehensive professional association of marketers. With over 45,000 members, the AMA has more than 500 chapters throughout North America. The AMA sponsors 25 major conferences per year, covering topics ranging from the latest trends in customer satisfaction measurement to business-to-business and service marketing, attitude research and sales promotion, and publishes nine major marketing publications.

For further information on the American Marketing Association, call toll free at 800-AMA-1150.

Or write to:

The American Marketing Association
311 South Wacker Drive
Suite 5800
Chicago, IL 60606-2266
Fax: 800-950-0872
URL: http://www.ama.org